P9-CIV-536

CHASING
THE TRUTH

**A Young Journalist's Guide to
Investigative Reporting**

CHASING THE TRUTH

A Young Journalist's Guide to Investigative Reporting

JODI KANTOR & MEGAN TWOHEY
Adapted by Ruby Shamir

PHILOMEL

PHILOMEL BOOKS
An imprint of Penguin Random House LLC, New York

First published in the United States of America by Philomel Books,
an imprint of Penguin Random House LLC, 2021

Visit us online at penguinrandomhouse.com.

Library of Congress Cataloging-in-Publication Data is available.

Printed in the USA

ISBN 9780593326992

10 9 8 7 6 5 4 3 2 1

CJKV

Edited by Jill Santopolo
Design by Ellice M. Lee
Text set in Sentinel

This is a work of nonfiction. Some names and identifying details have been changed.

TO OUR DAUGHTERS:
MIRA, TALIA, AND VIOLET

CONTENTS

NOTE TO READERS

Dear readers,

Welcome to our book and our partnership. In these pages, we're inviting you on a journey to find the truth, hear from people who had previously been silenced, and hold powerful wrongdoers accountable.

This is also an invitation into investigative journalism.

You're probably already immersed in general news coverage, reporting that accurately describes what's visible in the world around us. Presidential elections. Natural disasters. The deaths of notable public figures. This kind of journalism can connect us with other people's struggles and joys and make all of us witnesses to history. Many school papers include news reporting: on basketball games won or lost, or the appointment of a new principal.

Investigative reporting has a different goal: to uncover what's been hidden, to reveal injustice or other wrongdoing. It isn't about being an activist or advocating for a particular point of view—the only agenda is to follow the facts. Because facts are so powerful, this work can spur tremendous change. Over the years, investigative reporters have broken stories that have touched every aspect of our daily lives, spurring social movements, shifts in power, reforms, and greater safety. By investigating a break-in at the Watergate apartment complex in Washington, DC, Bob Woodward and Carl Bernstein revealed corruption that reached the highest levels of the White House and eventually brought down the Nixon presidency. We are proud that our investigation of harassment and abuse by the powerful Hollywood producer Harvey Weinstein fits into this tradition.

As you read this book, we want you to feel included and inspired. Maybe you don't know any reporters or authors or don't recognize many from backgrounds similar to yours. It's possible that you rarely encounter print newspapers in your community. Social media may be the main way that you and your friends get and share information. But young journalists can do investigative reporting as well. If you found that wealthy students were deploying test preparation and private counselors to an unfair advantage in college admissions, or that local elementary schools didn't have air-conditioning in the hot summers, or that the football team was hazing new members in abusive ways—those stories could light up discussion in your community and perhaps spur action.

In this book, we've tried to turn our work on Harvey Weinstein into a manual for this type of reporting. (To avoid confusion, we write about ourselves in the third person. In a first-person account of our reporting, which was collaborative but often involved us following separate threads, "I" could be either Jodi or Megan.)

Thank you for joining us for the duration of these pages, for puzzling through these events and clues as we have, for witnessing what we witnessed, and for hearing what we heard. We hope you feel welcome and that you'll consider a lifetime commitment to this work, as a journalist, a source, or a reader.

Jodi Kantor and Megan Twohey

INTRODUCTION

IN 2017 WOMEN had more power than ever before. The number of jobs once held almost exclusively by men—police officer, soldier, airline pilot—had narrowed almost to a vanishing point. Women led nations including Germany and the United Kingdom, and companies such as PepsiCo and the car manufacturer General Motors. In one year of work, it was possible for a thirtysomething-year-old woman to make more money than all of her female ancestors had made in their combined lifetimes.

But all too often, women were sexually harassed. Scientists, restaurant servers, cheerleaders, executives, and factory workers had to smile past unwanted touches or gropes, stares or leers, or unwelcome advances to get the next tip, paycheck, or raise. Sexual harassment was against the law—but it was also routine in some jobs. Women who spoke up were frequently dismissed or scorned. Victims were often hidden and isolated from one another. Their best option, many people agreed, was to accept money, usually in the form of a legal settlement, in exchange for silence—a promise that the victims would never out their abusers. The perpetrators, meanwhile, frequently sailed to ever-higher levels of success and praise. Harassers were often accepted, or even cheered, as mischievous bad boys.

On October 5, 2017, Jodi and Megan broke the story of alleged sexual harassment and abuse by Harvey Weinstein. Immediately, they watched with astonishment as a dam wall broke. Millions of women around the world told their own stories of mistreatment. Large numbers of men suddenly had to answer for their predatory behavior, and a new moment of accountability arose. For years, a shift had been slowly building, thanks to the efforts of pioneering feminists, legal scholars, other reporters, and activists like Tarana Burke, who had founded the #MeToo movement a decade before. But now a more sudden transformation was taking place.

In a world in which so much feels stuck, how does this sort of groundbreaking social change occur? Nothing about it had been inevitable or predicted. The only thing that was certain going into the Weinstein reporting was the process. To break this story, Jodi and Megan would rely on the tools of investigative journalism they had long used to write article after article.

When Megan was growing up, her mom was a producer at a local TV news station and her dad an editor at the *Chicago Tribune*. They would discuss current events around the dinner table, diving into the details behind the big headlines of the day. But as much as she enjoyed her close proximity to the profession, Megan didn't think she would become a journalist. She was raised in Evanston, Illinois, a racially diverse suburb of Chicago with a long commitment to civil rights, where students sang "Lift Every Voice and Sing," known as the Black national anthem, at school assemblies. Her environment instilled in her a passion for social justice, and she thought activism was the best way to pursue it. In high school, she was part of a walkout in response to a teacher's racist comment. In college, she helped organize a Take Back the Night rally to shine light on sexual violence and fight for safer conditions for female students. By taking to the streets, she hoped to illuminate problems and help spark reforms.

But by the time she graduated from college, Megan had started to also feel a pull toward journalism, inspired by an internship at ABC News's *Nightline*, which had shown her that high-quality broadcast journalism could have a big impact.

She eventually landed at the *Milwaukee Journal Sentinel* in Wisconsin covering local news like the county fair and police shootings. The assignments weren't glamorous, but they taught her how to report and write. With every article, she became more skilled and better able to take on bigger subjects. Her office was down the street from the local prison. She grew curious about what was happening behind its gates, started asking questions, and wrote stories exposing the mistreatment of female inmates. Later, while working in Chicago, she reported on abusive doctors and on police investigators who neglected to follow up on evidence they had collected.

Megan was thrilled that she was able to turn her questions about the world around her into reporting projects. And she was inspired by what was happening as a result. Her articles were triggering changes of policies and laws. The people she wrote about—inmates, patients, victims of crimes—were receiving more protections. It felt more rewarding than her earlier experiences with protesting. Rather than shout her opinions in the streets, she kept her head down, did research, collected documents, followed facts to uncover hidden truths.

One of her biggest discoveries came in 2012, after she had been working in journalism for more than a decade and a half. While reporting on adoptions of children from foreign countries, she stumbled on internet forums on Yahoo and Facebook, where parents complained that they no longer wanted their adopted children. "I am totally ashamed to say it but we do truly hate this boy!" one woman wrote of the eleven-year-old son she had adopted from Guatemala. "I would have given her away to a serial killer, I was so desperate," said another parent of her adopted daughter.

These parents weren't simply venting. They were actively offloading children. It was called "private re-homing," a term first used by people seeking new homes for their pets. Alarmed by what she found, Megan dug deeper.

In legal adoption proceedings, parents go through background checks, there are lawyers and courts involved to ensure the safety of the children, and all the parties have to comply with government regulations. But Megan discovered that after they adopted, it was remarkably easy for parents to get rid of kids they no longer wanted.

She began traveling the country and gathering accounts. Of parents who had given away their adopted sons and daughters, of families who had taken them in, and of the children who had been re-homed, sometimes multiple times. She was uncovering a secret, underground world, a lawless network, where children were sometimes transferred to adults with criminal backgrounds or histories of abuse and neglect.

Because no government agency oversaw or investigated or really even knew about—this practice, there was no way to figure out how widespread it was. The only data she had was based on her own analysis of one of the online forums she researched. She had reviewed thousands of advertisements for children and found that a child was offered to strangers on average once a week, most of the children had been adopted from overseas, and many were said to suffer from physical, emotional, or behavioral problems. There was a big, gaping hole in the child welfare system, and the most vulnerable children were falling through it.

To better understand the dangers, Megan tracked down one couple, Nicole and Calvin Eason, who had moved from state to state collecting these unwanted children, six of whom Megan had located. The parents who turned their adopted children over to the Easons didn't conduct background checks or know anything about them. But when Megan went to the police departments and child welfare agencies in the cities where the Easons had lived, she found public documents showing that Nicole's biological children had been removed from her care because she was a danger to them, that government officials determined that she and Calvin had "severe psychiatric problems" and "violent tendencies," and that the Easons faked a document certifying their parenting skills. When Megan interviewed Nicole, she casually admitted to hitting and threatening kids in her care.

Megan didn't know if all of her work would make a difference; she didn't know if anyone would pay attention. But she knew that the story had to be told and told right. She had to back up every word of her reporting with evidence and solid sourcing. And she had to treat the subjects of the story fairly and give them a chance to respond to the allegations, or accusations, against them. Nicole's statements denying claims made by the children appeared throughout the articles. And the parents who gave away their children were given space to defend their actions.

This work, meticulously researched and analyzed over a year and a half, eventually became a five-part series, revealing something that had never been exposed before and giving voice to children who had long been overlooked. After her series was published, several states immediately passed laws to protect children from re-homing. The Easons were investigated by the FBI and eventually convicted and sent to prison.

It also led to a new job for Megan, at the *New York Times*, where she sat a few cubicles away from a reporter almost exactly the same age named Jodi Kantor.

Unlike Megan, Jodi hadn't known any writers when she was growing up. As a kid in Staten Island, one of the outer boroughs of New York City, she had read nonstop, anything and everything in sight: newspapers, magazines, kids' books, adult fiction. If it had words, she was drawn to it. In some ways, the questions of investigative journalism suffused her childhood—Jodi was born thirty years after her grandparents were liberated from Nazi camps, and questions about what had really happened, and whether the victims would speak about their experiences, swirled around her family. And yet Jodi never imagined authoring books or even articles, much less tackling investigations. The idea that anyone would want to read what she wrote had seemed presumptuous. She read the *New York Times* every day while eating her after-school snack, even before she really understood what she was reading, but the journalists had seemed distant to her. They were mostly white men. When she read the work of women reporters, their names leapt out at her, and maybe planted a seed.

After graduating from college, Jodi enrolled in law school, to her family's pride. But a few weeks in, she realized she had to drop out. Journalism was what she loved, even if she hadn't done much of it, and if she didn't try it at age twenty-four, she never would. She became a magazine assistant, then an editor, and finally the person she'd never thought she would be: a writer with front-page bylines, narrating history as it unfolded, covering President Barack Obama and Michelle Obama for the *Times*.

But despite the heady assignment, and the importance of accurate, penetrating political coverage, there was something unsatisfying about the work, she felt. It was hard to see how a profile could change lives, and the political world felt artificial. Jodi wanted to question the way the world functioned—especially the world of work, particularly for women. She investigated gender discrimination at Harvard Business School, and employment practices at Amazon, and both organizations changed their policies after her stories were published (Amazon even granted its workers paid paternity leave for the first time).

In 2014, Jodi became obsessed with a widespread but mostly invisible technological change. The lives of hourly-wage workers were being torn apart by obscure but ubiquitous scheduling software that required them to report for duty at unpredictable hours. For fast food outlets and retail chains, the software was a big advantage, allowing them to summon workers whenever and wherever they needed. But that meant workers were scheduled for dreaded "clopenings," where they had to work the last shift until eleven p.m. when the store closed, then return the next morning at four a.m. to open again. The employees often found out about their weekly schedules only a couple of days in advance, or they would get sent home early on a slow day and lose wages they had been counting on. This was especially tough and disruptive for working parents who had to scramble last minute for babysitting and transportation, or cancel long-planned doctor's appointments and parent-teacher conferences for their kids.

The software, and the problems it created, were everywhere, a vast system causing untold problems for minimum-wage employees. Jodi talked to workers in malls, at restaurants, in person and on the phone, hearing nightmare anecdotes. But she wanted to write a story about one person who could stand for the whole nationwide mess. A few minutes into a phone conversation with Jannette Navarro, a barista at a San Diego Starbucks, she began calculating how soon she could get on an airplane headed west. Jannette was comfortable telling her story on the record. She was a character to root for, a devoted single mom of a young son. And as Jodi saw firsthand in San Diego, the algorithm determining her work hours, and the dreaded clopenings, was causing havoc in other parts of her life: compromising her ability to care for her son, straining her relationship with the aunt and uncle who had long helped her, and spurring Jannette and her boyfriend to break up. As Jodi documented these problems, she was clear with Jannette that she was there as a reporter, not an advocate. She wanted Jannette to trust her, but she didn't want Jannette to be misled about her intentions. So she kept her reporter's notebook visible at all times and often referenced the story she was writing.

Once back in New York, Jodi got to work on the next step of the story:

confirmations and comments. Jodi needed to make sure that whatever Jannette was telling her was true, which made for some awkward conversations with Jannette's aunt and uncle and ex-boyfriend about Jannette's personal history and fights they had had. But the part that Jodi was most concerned about was calling the executives at Starbucks. Just like Megan had done with the Easons, Jodi had to let the subjects of the story know exactly what she was planning to publish about them, positive or negative. In this case Jodi worried that Jannette's claims would anger company management and get her fired. Jodi had tiptoed so carefully that she had never even entered the San Diego Starbucks where Jannette worked. And now she was sharing Jannette's concerns about her job with her employers? The last thing Jodi wanted to do was further disrupt Jannette's life.

The first call she made to the company was just to confirm general details about its scheduling policy, without mentioning Jannette. Then, two days before the article was set to be published, she had an on-the-record conversation with an executive and encountered a new wrinkle. The Starbucks executive claimed that workers get at least one week of notice about their schedules, and typically two or three weeks. That set off an alarm in Jodi; she'd spoken to so many other workers whose experiences mirrored Jannette's. So Jodi went on a mad dash, contacting workers at seventeen Starbucks across the country. She had been right about the lack of notice, and the story was even more powerful because executives seemed so out of touch with what was actually happening in their shops.

A day after the story was published, Starbucks implemented policy changes, including eliminating clopenings and giving workers at least ten days of notice about their schedules. The story also helped launch a fair-scheduling movement across the country, and cities and states adopted rules to avoid situations like Jannette's.

Jodi was thrilled by the response, just as Megan had been when lawmakers acted to protect adopted children. But neither of them had taken sides. As reporters, they were in a pact with the public. Readers could trust their work because Megan and Jodi followed the facts wherever they led, without bias or an agenda, making the work fair and accurate. It didn't mean that the reporters were without emotions, but rather that their only goal was to pursue the truth. The First Amendment of the United States Constitution bans the government from making laws "abridging the freedom of speech, or of the press." The role of reporters is to ask questions of everyone, especially the powerful; to reveal abuses of power and violations of public trust; to document the facts with hard evidence and solid sources; and to be fair to all the parties involved. If a journalist is able to expose injustice in that manner, it can be hard to refute.

Jodi and Megan's Weinstein reporting took place at a time of accusations of "fake news," as the very notion of a national consensus on truth seemed to be fracturing. But the impact of the Weinstein revelations was so great in part because Jodi and Megan were able to establish so much evidence of wrongdoing. They documented a pattern of behavior based on first-person accounts, financial and legal records, company memos, and other revealing materials. In the wake of their work, there was little public debate about what Weinstein had done to women.

Weinstein, now a convicted rapist, has denied the allegations of nonconsensual sex in this book and has repeatedly asserted that our reporting is incorrect. "What you have here are allegations and accusations, but you do not have absolute facts," a spokesman said when we asked for a response to the revelations presented here.

This book is a detailed account of their investigation, its ups and downs, its winding paths and dead ends, its shaky start and shocking conclusion. It is an immersion in the techniques the reporters used to get this story out into the world, and it takes some measure of the result: an astounding shift in the lives of women in the US and beyond.

CHAPTER ONE

THE FIRST PHONE CALL

THE *NEW YORK* *Times* investigation into Harvey Weinstein began with the most promising source refusing even to get on the phone.

"Here's the thing, I have been treated quite shabbily by your paper at times and I believe the root of it is sexism," the actress Rose McGowan wrote on May 11, 2017, responding to an email from Jodi asking to talk. McGowan felt the *New York Times* discriminated against women and listed her criticisms: a speech she had made at a political dinner was covered in the Style section instead of the news pages. An earlier conversation she'd had with a *Times* reporter about Weinstein had been uncomfortable.

"The *NYT* needs to look at itself for sexism issues," she responded. "I'm not that inclined to help."

Months earlier, McGowan had accused an unnamed producer—rumored to be Weinstein—of rape, forcing her to have sex against her will. She had tweeted that she had been shamed while her rapist was praised. Now she was said to be writing a memoir intended to expose the entertainment industry's mistreatment of women.

Unlike almost anyone else in Hollywood, McGowan had a history of speaking out against sexism, even if it meant she wouldn't get movie roles. She once tweeted out the insulting clothing requirements on a casting notice for an Adam Sandler movie: "tank that shows off cleavage (push-up bras encouraged)." In general, her tone on social media was tough, confrontational: "It is okay to be angry. Don't be afraid of it," she had tweeted a month earlier, later adding: "dismantle the system." If McGowan, as much an activist as an actress, would not have one off-the-record conversation with Jodi, which would be kept confidential, who would?

Harvey Weinstein was not the man of the moment. In recent years, his moviemaking magic had faltered. But he still had power, specifically the power to make and boost careers. First he had invented himself, going from a modest upbringing in Queens, New York, to concert promotion to film distribution and production, and he seemed to know how to make everything around him bigger—films, parties, and most of all, people. Over and over, he had propelled young actors to stardom: Gwyneth Paltrow, Matt Damon, Michelle Williams, and Jennifer Lawrence. He could turn tiny independent movies into phenomena. He had pioneered the modern Oscar awards campaign, winning five Best Picture statues for himself and armloads for others. His record of raising money for Hillary Clinton, and joining her at countless fundraisers, was almost two decades long. When President Obama's daughter Malia had sought an internship in film, she worked for "Harvey"—first name only, used even by many strangers. By 2017, even though his movies were less successful than they used to be, his reputation remained outsized.

Rumors had long circulated about his treatment of women. But many people had dismissed the behavior, and nothing had ever been publicly documented. Other journalists had tried and failed in the past. A 2015 investigation by the City of New York Police Department (NYPD) into an accusation that he had groped—grabbed and touched—a woman against her will had ended without any criminal charges. "At some pt, all the women who've been afraid to speak out abt Harvey Weinstein are gonna have to hold hands and jump," Jennifer Senior, a journalist, had tweeted back then. Two years had passed. Nothing had happened. Jodi had heard that two more reporters, a writer at *New York* magazine and NBC's Ronan Farrow, had tried, but no stories had appeared.

In public, Weinstein boasted of feminist credentials, supporting causes and films that empowered women. Were the whispers about Weinstein's interactions with women wrong?

The point of the *Times* investigations department, tucked away from the hum of the rest of the newsroom, was to dig for what had never been reported, bringing to account people and institutions whose wrongdoings had been deliberately concealed. After Jodi did her initial research, the next step was often careful outreach. So how to reply to McGowan to motivate her to pick up the phone?

Her email had openings. First, she had written back. Lots of people never did. She had put thought into her note and cared enough to offer a critique. Maybe she was testing Jodi, jabbing at the *Times* to see if the reporter would defend it.

But Jodi wasn't looking to have an argument about her own work-place of fourteen years. Flattering McGowan ("I really admire the bravery of your tweets . . .") also was not the way to go. That would sap what little authority Jodi had in the interaction. And there was nothing to be said about the investigation to which McGowan would be contributing: if she asked how many other women Jodi had spoken to, the answer would be none.

The note would need to be phrased just so, with no mention of Weinstein's name: McGowan had a history of posting private communications on Twitter. She was someone who wanted to blow things open, but that impulse could backfire in this situation. ("Hey, world, check out this email from a *Times* reporter.") The subject matter made the response even trickier. McGowan had said she was an assault victim. Pressuring her would not be right.

In 2013, Jodi had started investigating women's experiences at corporations and other institutions, like the story about Jannette Navarro at Starbucks. The gender debate in the United States already seemed saturated with feeling: opinion columns, memoirs, expressions of outrage or sisterhood on social media. It needed more exposure of hidden facts. Especially about the workplace. Workers, from the lowliest to the most elite, were often afraid to question their employers. Reporters were not. In doing those stories, Jodi had found that gender was not just a topic but a kind of investigative entry point. Because women were still outsiders at many organizations, documenting what they experienced meant seeing how power functioned.

She wrote back to Rose McGowan, calling on those experiences:

> Here's my own track record on these issues: Amazon,
> Starbucks, and Harvard Business School have all
> changed their policies in response to gender-related
> problems I exposed. When I wrote about the class gap

in breastfeeding—white-collar women can pump on the job, lower-paid women cannot—readers responded by creating the first-ever mobile lactation suites, now available in 200+ locations across the country.

If you'd rather not speak, I understand, and best of luck with your book publication.

Thank you,
Jodi

McGowan wrote back within a few hours. She could talk anytime before Wednesday.

The call seemed like it could be tricky: McGowan appeared tough, with a buzz cut and that call-to-arms Twitter feed. But the voice on the phone belonged to someone impassioned and game who had a story and was searching for the right way to tell it. Her tweets about being raped had just been hints, with few details. Generally, the rule in interviews was that they were on the record, so the material could be published with the source's name unless otherwise discussed. But any woman with an assault complaint against Weinstein would probably be unwilling to have even an initial conversation. So Jodi agreed that the call would be kept private and off the record until they decided otherwise, and McGowan started in.

In 1997, she had been young and newly triumphant, on a heady trip to the Sundance Film Festival, where she alternated between premieres and parties, and a TV camera crew followed her around. She had only been in four or five films, but she was becoming one of the young starlets of the moment, with multiple new movies at the festival alone. Independent films were at the center of the culture, the festival was the place to be, and Harvey Weinstein was almighty. McGowan recalled the screening where she had sat right near Weinstein. Afterward, he had asked for a meeting with her, which made sense: the top producer wanted to get together with the rising star. She went to see him at the Stein Eriksen Lodge Deer Valley, in Park City, Utah, where they met in his room. Nothing happened except the usual talk about films and roles, she said.

But on the way out, Weinstein pulled her into a room and sexually assaulted her. She said she remembered feeling like she was leaving her body, floating up to the ceiling and observing the scene from above. "I was just feeling massive shock, I was going into survival mode," she said. She pretended she was having a good time as she thought of how to remove herself from the room. McGowan eventually got away from him, mentally giving herself step-by-step instructions: "Turn the door handle." "Walk out of this meeting."

Within a few days, she said, Weinstein had left a message on her home phone in Los Angeles with a creepy offer: other big female stars were his special friends, and she could join his club as well. Shocked and distraught, McGowan complained to her managers and hired a lawyer.

Lawyers represent clients in legal disputes. Defense lawyers represent the defendant, or accused, and plaintiffs' attorneys represent the plaintiff, or accuser. Oftentimes parties will agree to hammer out the terms of a settlement instead of going to court. The accused might agree to pay the accuser money, sometimes called "damages," and the accuser agrees to not pursue the case in open court. Both sides might sign confidentiality agreements as well, specifying that neither party is allowed to speak publicly of the matter. These nondisclosure agreements, or NDAs, are an effective way to bury an accusation—they often include a paragraph forbidding signers to even acknowledge the existence of the NDA.

Rose McGowan ended up with a $100,000 settlement from Weinstein—essentially, a payment to make the matter go away, without any admission of wrongdoing on his part—which she said she donated to a rape crisis center.

Jodi asked: Did she have her records from the settlement? As an investigative reporter, she needed to have documentation to corroborate, or support, McGowan's claims. "They never gave me a copy," she said.

The problem was worse than Weinstein, McGowan said. Hollywood was an organized system for abusing women. It lured them with promises of fame, turned them into highly profitable products, treated their bodies as property, required them to look perfect, and then discarded them. She claimed that many actresses were required to sign NDAs—the blanket agreements to stay silent about their true experiences. If they breathed a word about their experiences to anyone, they could get sued.

McGowan's comments were arresting. It wasn't new to say that Hollywood took advantage of women, forced them into conformity, and dumped them when they aged or rebelled. But hearing a direct account of exploitation from a familiar face, in full disturbing detail, and with one of the most renowned producers in Hollywood as the perpetrator, was entirely different: sharper, more specific, sickening.

The call ended with an agreement to talk again soon. The actress was an unusual character, but the sometimes outrageous things she had done or said or whom she had dated didn't matter for these purposes. The question was how her account would stand up to the rigors of the journalistic process, and, if it got that far, the inevitable challenge by Weinstein, and then public scrutiny. Before the *Times* would even consider publishing McGowan's allegations, they would need to be well supported and, finally, taken to Weinstein. He would have to be given an opportunity to respond.

The paper had a duty to be fair, especially given the gravity of the charges. In 2014, *Rolling Stone* magazine published an article about a horrific sexual assault at the University of Virginia without anything close to sufficient evidence. The ensuing controversy set off a series of lawsuits, almost ruined the magazine's reputation, and gave ammunition to those who said women invented stories of campus assault. The *Washington Post* reported that police had called the story "a complete crock," the *Columbia Journalism Review* called it "a mess," and the article won an "Error of the Year" award.

On first inspection, McGowan's account seemed vulnerable to challenge by Weinstein. He would easily be able to say that he remembered things differently, that she had appeared to enjoy herself in the hotel room. The old phone message was potentially significant, showing that Weinstein was using his power as a producer to force women to do what he wanted. But unless McGowan had the kept the recording from two decades ago, it was just a memory of a long-ago phone message, also easy to deny.

As a sole account, McGowan's story had a high likelihood of

becoming a classic "he said, she said" dispute. McGowan would tell a terrible story. Weinstein would deny it. With no witnesses, people would take sides, Team Rose versus Team Harvey.

But McGowan said she had gotten a settlement. Finding any record of it would be difficult, but there had been lawyers, a signed agreement, money that changed hands, the donation to the rape crisis center. The agreement had to be documented somewhere. It wouldn't prove what had happened in the hotel room, but it could add support by showing that Weinstein had paid McGowan a significant sum at the time to settle a dispute.

Jodi brought everything she had learned to her longtime editor at the *Times*, Rebecca Corbett, who was an expert in complex investigations. They discussed whether McGowan's account could be backed up, and the important question: Did other women have similar stories about him?

Finding that out would require huge effort. Weinstein had produced or distributed hundreds of movies over the decades. With his brother, Bob, he had co-owned and run two companies: Miramax and The Weinstein Company (TWC), his current business. That meant there were a lot of potential sources, a better situation than when critical information was held by just a few people. But there was an overwhelming number of people to contact, actresses and former employees scattered across several continents, most of whom probably wouldn't want to talk.

In mid-June Corbett suggested that Jodi contact a colleague, Megan Twohey, who was relatively new at the paper. Megan had recently had a baby and was on maternity leave, but she had a real touch with this kind of work, the editor said. Jodi didn't know what help she would be, but she sent off an email anyway.

When Megan got Jodi's email, she was caring for her newborn child and recovering from the most bruising reporting stretch of her career. She had arrived at the *Times* in February 2016 to cover politics, investigating the presidential candidates, Republican Donald Trump and Democrat Hillary Clinton. Megan had said yes to the job with some hesitation: politics had never been her assignment or interest.

Within weeks of her arrival, Dean Baquet, the executive editor of the paper—the top journalist, responsible for the whole newspaper—had tapped Megan for a specific line of inquiry that drew on her reporting expertise, uncovering sex crimes and sexual misconduct. Baquet had already enlisted another reporter, Michael Barbaro, to investigate Trump's treatment of women, and Baquet wanted him and Megan to answer the question of whether Trump's behavior toward women ever crossed legal or ethical lines.

Their first article on the subject—which included allegations of harassing, abusive, and violent behaviors—was published at dawn on Saturday, May 14, 2016, and it quickly exploded, eventually becoming the most-read *Times* political article thus far that year. Before publication, Megan and Barbaro had conducted a lengthy interview of the candidate and woven in his responses, including his denials of any misconduct and his insistence that he had always treated women with respect.

Trump and his supporters were enraged about the piece and came out swinging, taking direct shots at Megan and Barbaro on social media, in emails, in angry phone calls. Bill O'Reilly, the bombastic king of right-wing news, took to the airwaves to tell millions of viewers not to trust her work. "The problem is, Megan Twohey is a feminist, or so it seems," he said. His argument was absurd—as the *Washington Post* asked, should a male chauvinist, someone who believes women are inferior to men, report the story?—but O'Reilly used the full force of his influence to blunt the impact of the findings and to try to discredit her.

When Megan and Barbaro wrote a second piece, highlighting the stories of two more women who accused Trump of unwanted touching and kisses, it too provoked an angry reaction. Megan had reached out to Trump's staff for comment. Instead she got a furious phone call directly from Trump. He seethed on the line and accused the women of lying. He threatened to sue the *New York Times* if it published their accounts.

Trump's lawyer sent a letter to Baquet demanding that he retract the stories of the women. David McCraw, vice president and assistant general counsel of the *New York Times*—one of its top lawyers—beloved in the newsroom for his unflappability and protection of journalists, replied with equal force. It's illegal for news publications to libel people—invent and publish lies about them, to defame them, on purpose. This article, however, was well researched, sourced, and documented, and Trump couldn't refute it. Public figures don't get to sue simply because they don't like the truth reporters have uncovered.

"It would have been a disservice not just to our readers but to democracy itself to silence their voices," the lawyer wrote.

He all but dared Trump to sue the *Times*. "If he believes that American citizens had no right to hear what these women had to say and that the law of this country forces us and those who would dare criticize him to stand silent or be punished, we welcome an opportunity to have a court set him straight."

It was a rousing defense, not just of journalism but of the rights of women to make allegations against powerful men. When the *Times* published the letter on its website, it went viral immediately.

But inside the newsroom, Megan was afraid Trump would follow through with a lawsuit against her, Barbaro, and the paper, as McCraw suspected he would if he wasn't elected. Trump would ultimately lose in court, but it would be a long, difficult legal process. Megan had begun preserving all of her notes, emails, and text messages, in case of future legal discovery; for a lawsuit, she would need to hand over every bit of evidence to the court. But that never came to be. Instead, in November 2016, Trump was elected president.

In April, following the 2016 election, Megan and Jodi each watched, with astonishment, a series of developments that would lead directly to the beginning of the Weinstein investigation. Bill O'Reilly, the television host at the peak of his power who had gone after Megan and her feminism, lost his position at the Fox News network, which was known for its right-wing shows, after the *Times* exposed how he and the company had covered up repeated allegations of sexual harassment. The article, by Emily Steel and Michael Schmidt, had taken eight months to report, and it proved that O'Reilly had racked up settlements with at least five women who had accused him of verbal abuse, lewd remarks, and unwanted come-ons. O'Reilly and Fox News had handed over what then looked like a total of $13 million to silence the women: an enormous secret payout from one of America's top critics of feminism.

In that story, only a single woman had spoken on the record about her allegations: Wendy Walsh, a former guest who lost a lucrative offer to be a regular contributor on O'Reilly's show after she declined an invitation back to his hotel suite. Most of the women in the story were prevented from speaking because they had settled with O'Reilly or the network. They had accepted large sums of money in exchange for agreeing never to talk about what had happened.

But Steel and Schmidt had realized something important: transactions that complex can never be truly secret. The agreements involved lawyers, negotiations, and money, and others inevitably found out too—colleagues, agents, family members, and friends. Together the payments formed a legal and financial trail that told the story of the allegations against O'Reilly. The settlements didn't prevent the story; they were the story, a tale of cover-ups that illuminated the alleged wrongdoing. This was a new way of reporting on sexual harassment.

Within days, big companies like Mercedes-Benz and Allstate stopped buying advertisements on O'Reilly's show. Most important, other women at Fox started lodging complaints about the host's behavior. On April 19, not even three weeks after the publication of the *Times* story, he was fired. Both he and Roger Ailes, the Republican power broker and architect of the Fox network, had lost their jobs, not due to claims of mistreating women—Fox had known about many of those—but rather because of public exposure to those claims. It was like a momentary reversal in the physics of power.

Times editors quickly took the measure of the moment. Many women seemed increasingly fed up, first with the presidential election, and now with the revelations about O'Reilly. Convincing women to go on the record on matters like these was never simple, but this could be a rare window of opportunity.

The O'Reilly story offered a playbook. Almost no one ever came forward completely on their own. But if patterns of bad behavior could be revealed, there might be a way to tell more of these stories. The editors put together a team of reporters to look at a range of industries, like the tech industry, a field supposedly unbound by old rules, which nonetheless excluded women. Academia—universities and colleges—also seemed ripe for investigation because of the power that professors held over graduate students who wanted careers in the same fields. The journalists also planned to focus on low-income workers who had low visibility, who were afraid to lose their jobs if they complained about harassment.

A few days after O'Reilly was fired, Rebecca Corbett asked Jodi to pursue the answers to two questions. The first was, were there other powerful men in American life covering up abusive behavior toward women? Jodi had quietly made some calls for advice, and Shaunna Thomas, co-founder and head of a feminist group called UltraViolet, had suggested that Jodi look to Hollywood, Rose McGowan's upcoming book, and Harvey Weinstein. But Corbett also gave Jodi a second assignment: to go beyond individual wrongdoers and pin down the elements, the system, that kept sexual harassment so widespread and hard to address. How common were these settlements, which seemed to pop up in every story, and how had they masked the problem?

When Jodi phoned for advice, Megan still did not know what stories she would pursue once she returned from maternity leave. But they discussed what had motivated the women in Megan's stories about Trump to come forward and how the O'Reilly article had become proof that the *Times* knew how to execute a project this delicate without a hitch. They analyzed what to say in the very first seconds of a phone call with a stranger who might be a victim, and Megan suggested a few new approaches, including one she had used when getting sexual assault victims in Chicago to share their experiences: "I can't change what happened to you in the past, but together we may be able to use your experience to help protect other people."

That sentence clicked like nothing else had. It did not overpromise or suck up. It suggested compelling reasons to risk talking about a painful, messy subject. It was what Jodi had been trying to say to McGowan in that initial email: we mean business.

The pitch was about helping other people. This was always the truest, best reason to talk to a journalist, and one of the only potent answers to "I don't want the attention" or "I don't need the stress."

After that phone call, Jodi had a question for Corbett: How soon would Megan be back from maternity leave?

CHAPTER TWO

HOLLYWOOD SECRETS

MEGAN'S ADVICE WAS valuable, but as the Weinstein investigation continued in June 2017, the daunting question was how to even get top actresses on the phone. The typical procedure to reach these stars was to call their publicists, whose jobs were to make sure the actresses got good press. But that was out of the question, as was contacting agents and managers who helped them land movie roles. Those people were paid to build and maintain barriers. They were often loyal to power brokers like Weinstein because when their clients scored parts in his movies they got a cut of the payments. Besides, the questions were private, too awkward to share with paid intermediaries. Jodi's only hope was to connect directly with actresses. But she wasn't sure she knew a single one: it was a world in which she had virtually no sources or connections.

Jodi clicked through red-carpet photos from the recent Cannes Film Festival in France. As usual, there were few shots of men. Nicole Kidman, Jessica Chastain, Salma Hayek, Charlize Theron, and Marion Cotillard posed for the cameras; Uma Thurman stood in a glittering gold skirt at a charity event annually championed by Weinstein, a black-tie party and auction for the American Foundation for AIDS Research, or amfAR. Was it possible that any of them had been Weinstein victims? What did they know about the experiences of others? The women looked flawless, serene, and hopelessly out of reach.

She began seeking private email addresses and phone numbers for women who had appeared in Weinstein's films—especially Ashley Judd, who had given an interview to *Variety* in 2015, in which she had described being sexually harassed by a producer. Some of the searches for contact information practically turned into full investigations themselves: calls to relatives who were listed in public phone records; searches for go-betweens who might make introductions.

The few times Jodi got actresses on the phone, the conversations were mostly short and unproductive. Jodi emailed Judith Godrèche, a famous French actress who complained privately about Weinstein's abuse. No reply. She tried again and got a note back. "I am so sorry, my lawyer doesn't want me to be involved," Godrèche wrote. A frustrating response, but also a clue: Involved in what?

Contacting Weinstein's former employees was a little more fruitful.

They were certainly more reachable, on LinkedIn or at their office numbers or homes. Their responses fell into conflicting categories. Many sounded unsurprised to hear from a reporter but still refused to speak. Others were willing to provide bits and pieces: old suspicions that had lingered across the years; guidance on which Hollywood stars to try to reach.

Some of the former employees gave lectures: Harvey Weinstein's private life was his private business. The practice of actresses submitting to producers and directors in exchange for roles was as old as Hollywood itself, an unpleasant but permanent part of the business, they said. Several used the same phrase to describe how Weinstein had treated actresses: "Oh, he may have chased her around a couch," they said of this or that woman as if they were describing a pantomime. Those former employees spoke to Jodi as if she were a naive idealist. Weinstein's treatment of women had been an open secret for years, they said. Jodi would never get the story, and even if she did, no one would care.

Slowly, Jodi began to reach a few well-known actresses, through a mutual friend here, an unusually helpful manager there. Some of their email addresses were pseudonyms, often comical ones, and once they had connected, they swore Jodi to secrecy. But they were direct.

Hollywood was plagued by rampant sexual abuse, most of them said. Jodi met with the actress Marisa Tomei. She wasn't a Weinstein victim, but she shared a theory that Hollywood was caught in a vicious cycle: girls admired and modeled themselves after the fantasy women onscreen. Those women couldn't then describe the harassment or the punishing physical standards; that would be self-sabotage. So the cycle continued with the next generation of girls growing up with Hollywood dreams and little understanding that the industry could mistreat them too. Daryl Hannah, her voice familiar from years of hit movies but filled with anxiety, said that she had been victimized by Weinstein but felt too fearful to go into any detail. Another actress, an Oscar winner, said she had wanted to see him stopped for years but hadn't really known how to help, because the fellow actresses who had confided in her about their encounters wanted their privacy protected. This woman had tracked the failed reporting efforts years earlier at the *New Yorker* and the stalled *New York* magazine article and wondered why every story in the works seemed to disappear.

The conversations with these actresses would not be made public, but they were telling, contradicting the lectures about how Weinstein was a nonstory. Tomei and the others had global success, important roles, awards. They were insiders, but on this topic, they felt they had little ability to spur change, and they wanted the *Times* investigation to succeed.

When Jodi reached out to a few other women they had suggested, nothing came of it: everyone said no. Soon even some of the actresses who had been helpful stopped responding to Jodi's emails and texts.

The same week she met with Tomei, Jodi received a promising email. Lisa Bloom, a celebrity feminist lawyer and the daughter of famed women's rights attorney Gloria Allred, wanted to talk. She had represented women in some of the most important and high-profile male misconduct cases, including against Bill O'Reilly. Jodi figured that Bloom had clients with allegations against Weinstein, had caught wind of the *Times* project, and was getting in touch to help.

Jodi forwarded the email to her colleague Emily Steel, one of the reporters who had broken the story about Bill O'Reilly's settlements. Jodi had quickly learned to listen to everything Steel said. As soon as she got the email, Steel called with a warning. Bloom was in business with Weinstein, she said. The information was public. Bloom had posted a gushing tweet a few months before: "BIG ANNOUNCEMENT: My book SUSPICION NATION is being made into a miniseries, produced by Harvey Weinstein and Jay Z!"

Jodi realized the person behind the email wasn't Bloom. Harvey

Weinstein knew what the *Times* was working on, and he was going on the offensive.

There had been no obligation for Jodi to give Weinstein notice of the investigation—it wasn't even clear that there would be a story yet—and the duty to ask him for an interview or responses would come later. But now that he knew, it would make the reporting even more difficult. Any investigation into serious wrongdoing was a contest with its subject to control information, to get to sources—a race to expose on the reporters' end, a race to hide on the other.

She would have liked a little more running room, but there was nothing to do but to keep reporting. Jodi arranged a call with Bloom and kept it short, saying little.

Nicholas Kristof, the *Times* opinion columnist, made getting in touch with Ashley Judd simple. He had written the foreword for her autobiography. Days after he made an introduction, Jodi was on FaceTime with Judd, who had already figured out the reason for the call. And unlike Tomei, she had a personal story to tell about Weinstein.

In 1996, when Judd was in her late twenties, becoming a star in films including *Heat* and *A Time to Kill*, she had met Weinstein at a Los Angeles event. The producer had asked to get together, and Judd had assumed they would have a business conversation. They planned to meet at the Beverly Hills Hotel—at the Polo Lounge restaurant there, Judd presumed. She suspected nothing. Her father was on the trip, and she had introduced the two older men at the event. "My own dad didn't see it coming," Judd said.

When she arrived at the hotel, she was directed to meet Weinstein in a suite, where he had a bottle of champagne on ice. She took only a few sips. They made small talk, and "I got myself out of there as fast as I could," she remembered, a little suspicious about what he wanted.

Days later, he issued another invitation, this time to a breakfast meeting at the Peninsula Hotel in Beverly Hills. A conversation so early in the morning would surely be safe, Judd reasoned.

She arrived at the hotel exhausted. She had been up all night filming her first big thriller, *Kiss the Girls*, with Morgan Freeman, and had come straight from the set. When the reception staff told her that she would be meeting with the producer in his suite, instead of the restaurant, she was annoyed: she needed sleep, and room service would likely take forever to arrive. She figured she would order cereal to save time.

When she arrived at the room, she recalled to Jodi, Weinstein was in a bathrobe, which was not what she expected. He wanted to give her a massage. She refused. He countered by suggesting a shoulder rub. She rejected that too. Next he steered her toward a closet, asking her to help pick out his clothing for the day. Then toward the bathroom. Two decades later, she could still picture the layout of the hotel room, she said.

Weinstein's requests turned even more overtly sexual, she said. She refused each one, but he kept going. "I said no, a lot of ways, a lot of times, and he always came back at me with some slimy ask," she said. His movements were almost like military commands, she told Jodi, with a chop-chop quality: first you go here, and then you go there.

She recalled feeling trapped in the room and fearful of hurting her work prospects. She needed an exit strategy, a way of getting away from Weinstein. Judd said she had been in a no-win situation: to reject the producer was to risk career consequences. So she had quickly come up with a joke that wouldn't offend him while finding a way to leave safely.

At the time, Judd mentally classified it as a creepy incident. Soon after, she described what happened to her mother, the singer Naomi Judd; her father; her agent; and later on, other confidantes. Judd had sounded calm during the call with Jodi, and maybe that was why: she had not hidden her story, so there was little confessional rawness to her telling.

A few years later, while filming *Frida*, Judd told its star, Salma Hayek, and another actress, Valeria Golino, about what had happened with Weinstein. That's his thing, they said. He was always making those kinds of requests. He had done similar things to them too.

Judd asked the others why the women weren't banding together to stand up to Weinstein. "I didn't understand how any of us could be so scared of him," Judd said. But the movie *Frida* was Hayek's labor of love, it was being made by Weinstein, and he had the power to stop production at any moment.

During the hour-long call with Judd, the investigation shifted a little. Judd had described a group of actresses who, years earlier, had identified Weinstein's troubling behavior. He was a powerful boss who used the excuse of business meetings to try to pressure women into sexual interactions, she said, and no one did anything about it.

Loneliness had defined Ashley Judd's upbringing. Born in 1968 with the name Ashley Ciminella, her parents had split early. Her mother was then an amateur musician who worked as a waitress and then a secretary to pay the bills, and Ashley attended thirteen schools in four states before graduating from high school, each time losing friends. Growing up, she had been abused several times. She told the adults who were supposed to be looking after her, but they didn't believe her. One summer in high school, when she worked as a model in Japan, she was sexually assaulted, she said.

But at the University of Kentucky, she found female companionship in a sorority and gender studies courses, and she discovered a taste for activism, leading a student walkout to protest a trustee's racial remark. She thought of becoming a Christian missionary, and she applied and was accepted to the Peace Corps, which she intended to join after graduation.

But she became an actor instead—she wanted to try it while she was young and could take chances—and then a star. Still, in her free time, she used her celebrity for advocacy work, visiting poor villages and clinics all over the world to draw attention to the disease AIDS, violence against women, and women's health care. Despite the problems Judd had seen in Hollywood, she kept her two lives, in entertainment and public health causes, separate.

In 2009, at the age of forty-one, she enrolled in a midcareer master's program at Harvard's Kennedy School. In a course called Gender Violence, Law, and Social Justice, the professor Diane Rosenfeld argued that the legal system had been constructed to protect men more than women. In contrast, she introduced students to research on the behavior of bonobo apes, who over the course of evolution have eliminated male sexual pressure in their communities. If a male does get aggressive toward a female bonobo, she lets out a special cry, Rosenfeld explained. The other females come to her aid, descending from the trees and fending off the attacker.

For Judd, the class was a revelation. She channeled her thoughts into a final paper that called for women to recognize their common experiences and take on sexual aggression. "I propose a model based on female-female alliances," she wrote on the first page. She wanted women to follow the example of the bonobos, becoming less separate and secretive, joining together to chase away overly aggressive men.

It would be hard to convince women that things could change, she wrote in her research paper, which won a Dean's Scholar Award. "Bias is built into the very structures of our formal institutions, economy, and daily life," she said. But "something is waiting on the other side." What was needed, she wrote, was a "bold step of trust that breaks isolation."

Still, in June 2017, Judd was not sure if she wanted to accuse Weinstein publicly. She had already tried to call out his behavior once. In 2015, she had given that account to *Variety* magazine, without naming Weinstein, Hayek, or Golino, hoping it would spark something, maybe a surge of others coming together.

Nothing much happened. Any attention was directed at Judd, not Weinstein, and it was brief and sensationalized. To come forward again might repeat that experience.

This was a cautionary tale. Judd's account in *Variety* had been gutsy, but it was a lone account without a perpetrator's name or any supporting information. Impact in journalism came from specificity—names, dates, proof, and patterns. Jodi didn't want Judd to decline to participate in what might be a much stronger story because a weaker one had gone nowhere.

Judd had reason to be wary. But on the call, Jodi had used a word she had been waiting to hear: "pattern." An important factor for her, Judd said, would be how many other stories the reporters were able to track down and whether other actresses were going on the record. True to her Harvard paper, she wanted to be one of many women standing up to Weinstein in unison.

The call ended with a plan: Judd was going to reach out to Salma Hayek. Jodi also connected with Lena Dunham and her producing partner on the television show *Girls*, Jenni Konner. They had heard stories about Weinstein's alleged predatory behavior and had wanted to expose him in Lenny Letter, their online newsletter, but they didn't have the investigative or legal resources to defend themselves should Weinstein sue them. Dunham, who had served as a speaker and supporter for Hillary Clinton during the 2016 campaign, told Jodi she had told Clinton's aides to stop relying on Weinstein as a fundraiser, but her warnings went nowhere. After the revelations became public, Clinton and her team expressed shock and denied the extent of Dunham's warning.

Konner and Dunham became a two-women celebrity switchboard, sending Jodi some of the direct contact information she needed, working quickly and discreetly. Another entertainment executive with a feminist bent did the same.

The response rate from the actresses was still low. But by the end of June, Konner had news: Gwyneth Paltrow wanted to talk.

At the outset, Paltrow had barely been on Jodi's list of people to contact. She had been Weinstein's golden girl, one of his top stars, and twenty years later, the memories of her acting career were still tied to him. They had been photographed together many times, a laughing father-daughter-like pair. In 1999, when Paltrow won the Oscar for Best Actress for her role in *Shakespeare in Love*, Weinstein stood next to her, radiating pride: he had made the movie, molded the star. Back then, Paltrow's nickname had been First Lady of Miramax. She seemed unlikely to help the *Times*. She was hardly a rebel like McGowan or an activist like Judd. She had become a health-and-beauty entrepreneur, and for some people, a love-to-hate figure.

But once their phone call was scheduled, for the final weekend of June 2017, Paltrow cut a different figure: she was a dead-center source who might know more than anyone yet. On the telephone, Paltrow was polite and sounded a little jittery. After the ritual reassurances—yes, this was off the record; yes, Jodi understood the delicacy of the situation—Paltrow shared the unknown side of the story of her relationship with Weinstein.

They had met by an elevator at the Toronto Film Festival in 1994 or '95, when she was around twenty-two, Paltrow recalled. At that point, she barely had a career. Her parents, the actress Blythe Danner and Bruce Paltrow, a director and producer, were successful, and she had gotten encouraging reviews in a film called *Flesh and Bone*, but she was still auditioning for more parts.

Right there at the elevator, Weinstein gave her his vote of confidence. *I saw you in that movie; you have to come work for us*, she remembered him saying. *You're really talented.* "I just remember feeling legitimized by his opinion," she said.

Before too long, he offered her two films. If she would do a comedy called *The Pallbearer*, Weinstein said, she could also have the lead in his upcoming adaptation of Jane Austen's *Emma*—a dream job, a star-making role.

Paltrow joined the downtown Miramax fold, which at that time struck her as warm and creative. "I felt like I was home," she said. She was dating Brad Pitt, who was far more famous than she at the time, and flying between New York and Los Angeles. On one of those trips, before shooting started for *Emma*, she got a fax from her representatives at Creative Artists Agency telling her to meet Weinstein at the Peninsula Hotel in Beverly Hills.

That was the same hotel as in Judd's story. What Paltrow said next also felt familiar. The meeting seemed routine, held in a suite for privacy. "I bounced up there, I'm sort of like a golden retriever, all happy to see Harvey," she said. They talked business. But Weinstein closed by placing his hands on her and asking to go into the bedroom and exchange massages. Paltrow could barely process what was happening, she said. She had thought of Weinstein as an uncle. The thought that he was interested in her sexually shocked her and made her feel queasy. He asked a second time to move into the bedroom, she said.

She excused herself, but "not so he would feel he had done something wrong," she said. As soon as she left, she told Brad Pitt what had happened, then a few friends, family members, and her agent.

The next part of Paltrow's story was different from Judd's and made it potentially more consequential. Weeks later, when Paltrow and Pitt attended the same theater premiere as Weinstein, Pitt confronted the producer and told him to keep his hands to himself. At the time, Paltrow felt relieved: her boyfriend was her protector.

But when she returned to New York, Weinstein called and threatened her, yelling at her for telling Pitt what had happened. "He said some version of *I'm going to ruin your career*," she said. She remembered standing in her old apartment on Prince Street in SoHo, fearful she would lose the two roles, especially the starring one in *Emma*. "I was nothing, I was a kid, I was signed up. I was petrified, I thought he was going to fire me," she said.

She tried to put the relationship back on professional footing, explaining to Weinstein that telling her boyfriend had been natural, but that she wanted to put the episode behind them and move forward. "I always wanted peace, I never wanted any problem," she said. For a time, their relationship was restored. "In this funny way, I was like, well, that's behind us," she said. The more successful her partnership with Weinstein became, the less she felt she could say about the ugly episode at the start of their collaboration. "I had this incredible career there," she said. "I was expected to keep the secret."

The ethos of Hollywood, she said, was to swallow complaints and to put up with exactly that kind of behavior. She didn't think about the encounter as part of something larger or more systemic, so deeply embedded in how Hollywood worked. During her years with Miramax, she heard the occasional disturbing rumor about Weinstein, but never with specifics attached. Weinstein was abusive in other ways that made the moment in the bedroom seem mild in comparison. He threw things. His explosive anger and yelling fits were beyond anything Paltrow or others had seen from a grown man. The Miramax employees she knew lived in fear of his hot-headedness. "It's the H-bomb, the H-bomb is coming," they would warn before he approached.

After two Miramax movies starring Paltrow tanked—*Bounce* in 2000 and *View from the Top* in 2003—Weinstein's treatment of her changed, she said. "I wasn't the golden girl with the Midas touch," she said. "My worth had diminished in his eyes." By the time Paltrow was pregnant with her first child, she quietly distanced herself from the producer.

That remained the case until 2016, when Miriam Weinstein, the producer's mother and a beloved figure at Miramax, passed away, and Paltrow wrote Weinstein a brief condolence email. To her shock, he read it aloud at the funeral and called her soon afterward—to thank her, Paltrow figured.

But after the niceties, he began to pressure her again. *New York* magazine was working on an exposé of his treatment of women. They have nothing, Weinstein told Paltrow. He wanted her to promise that she wouldn't talk about the incident at the Peninsula all those years before. "I just really want to protect the people who did say yes," he said, meaning women who had given in to his advances. Paltrow declined the magazine's interview request, but she avoided saying whether she would ever speak.

The story needed to come out, she said to Jodi. For a long time, she had assumed she would never disclose what had happened. But twenty years later, everything looked different, and that's why she was on the phone now. Paltrow made it clear that she was a long way from going on the record.

She was not having a good public relations moment, to put it mildly. At the time, her e-commerce business and lifestyle brand, Goop, was under heavy criticism for selling wellness products with dubious or no health benefits. On Instagram, Paltrow looked as untroubled as ever. Privately, she was feeling crushed and unsure if she could handle any more controversy. She was certain that any story involving her, Weinstein, and sex was likely to be sensationalized, turned into the trashy celebrity scandal of the week. "I didn't know if I was going to be dragged through the mud," she said. "That's usually what happens to women if you look, historically." More than a hundred people were working for her, paying mortgages and raising children, and wading into more controversy could hurt them too. "I can't wreck the business," as she put it.

But Paltrow decided that she would use her Hollywood network to help Jodi identify and enlist other Weinstein victims so the women could share the burden of speaking up together. (Jodi couldn't mention Judd to her or vice versa.) Paltrow listed a half dozen other famous names she wanted to call, asking for pointers on the protocols of investigative journalism. Jodi suggested others. Paltrow was on vacation with her children in Europe, and her social media feeds showed wine glasses, a picnic, and an Italian lake. Privately, she also was texting old costars and acquaintances for so-and-so's contact information, asking other women if they would speak.

On July 5, Megan returned to the *Times*, undecided about what to cover. On that first day, Rebecca Corbett spelled out Megan's options. The first was to return to Donald Trump. In the final months of her pregnancy, Megan had started scrutinizing Trump's company and ties to Russia, turning up his pursuit of a Trump Tower Moscow during the presidential race and other questionable dealings. The second was to join the investigation of Harvey Weinstein. Jodi was still eager for Megan to join her. Was she interested?

Megan took a day to think about it, seeking the advice of a few trusted colleagues. Those who covered Trump were firm: Trump was the story of a lifetime. Much more important than a sleazy Hollywood producer accused of preying on young actresses. Passing up the chance to report on the president would be a huge mistake. But Megan wasn't so sure; she had watched hard-hitting articles about Trump pile up without much impact.

However, the Weinstein investigation was a question mark. The McGowan accusation was grave, but some of the material Jodi had gathered didn't seem that awful compared to the sex crimes Megan had reported in Chicago. How much harm was really involved in the massage stories? She had a hard time imagining famous actresses as a category of victims. A prime mission of journalism was to give voice to those who were often ignored. Movie stars, with their fame and fortune, were far from that.

Did what happened to these women even meet the legal definition of sexual harassment? The women were not technically employees of Weinstein, and for some of them, there were no specific movie roles on the line. How much could this investigation really prove?

But, Jodi insisted, if the accounts were accurate, Weinstein personified the way powerful men could abuse their status to establish dominance over women. When he had invited these women to meetings, they had responded because they wanted to work, because they had ambition, creativity, and hopes and dreams. In return, he put them in no-win positions: submit to sexual demands or risk consequences.

That was sexual harassment, whether or not it met the legal definition. The claims against Weinstein appeared to have a predatory edge. And that his accusers were famous women was part of the point: it proved this was a universal problem.

Megan pulled up a seat at Jodi's cubicle and got to work.

Now both reporters were reaching out to some of the most prominent women in the world. Angelina Jolie had a Weinstein story, they heard from a former Miramax employee. Jodi got her email address from the helpful Hollywood executive, sent the star a carefully worded note, spoke to an adviser, and waited to see if she might participate. They also wrote to Uma Thurman: she did not reply, the reporters discovered later, because someone had told her they were not trustworthy. Despite repeated notes, Salma Hayek never responded either.

Ambra Battilana Gutierrez, an Italian model, had allegedly been groped by Weinstein during a meeting at his office in 2015 and reported the incident to the police in New York. The police investigated.

Those who engage in sexual misconduct can be held legally accountable in two different ways. Sexual abuse and assaults can be prosecuted in criminal court by government lawyers. Those found guilty often go to prison. Sexual harassment, and some other offenses, are violations of civil law, meaning the victim can sue the accused for money. But the cases may also be settled without a lawsuit ever being filed in court, often with the accused agreeing to pay the victim as part of a secret settlement.

In the end, the district attorney's office did not begin criminal proceedings against Weinstein, but working with undercover detectives,

Gutierrez had apparently recorded the producer discussing what had happened.

Megan wasn't hearing back from the model, and the New York Police Department was refusing to provide her with a copy of the incident report under a long-standing policy that prohibited the release of such records. So she called around to attorneys and others who might have knowledge of the case. While reporting on a different story in Chicago, Megan had interviewed Linda Fairstein, renowned in the field of sex crimes prosecution. Now Megan reached out to Fairstein again, hoping she might have valuable insight into the same sex crimes division where she had once worked, the one that had declined to press charges. But as soon as she heard the reason for the call, Fairstein's tone turned cool. Ambra Battilana Gutierrez's allegations had been unfounded, she insisted. There was no criminal conduct there. And there wasn't anything irregular about how the case was handled. "I don't think there's a road to go down," she told Megan.

In mid-July, the reporters met in person for the first time with Rose McGowan—over dinner at Jodi's apartment, for privacy. McGowan was anything but relaxed. Her eyes darted around the room. She had no interest in small talk. But she gamely answered question after question, especially about the aftermath of the hotel room encounter and who else might remember it or provide evidence. Jodi and Megan asked her to try to obtain a copy of her settlement agreement, explaining that one of the law firms must have retained a copy.

After the interview with McGowan, the reporters mentioned one particularly confusing question to Matt Purdy, a top editor at the paper who had overseen the O'Reilly story, pulled together the broader sexual harassment team, and was keeping a close eye on the investigation. Beyond McGowan, some secondary sources were also suggesting that Weinstein had repeatedly committed criminal offenses: assault, rape. Should the reporters concentrate on finding those claims, prioritizing the most serious kinds of potential violations? Not necessarily, Purdy said: concentrate first on what you can prove, even if what you can prove are lesser offenses. Get the women's allegations of sexual harassment on the record, the documents, and especially the settlements paid to victims. No one had ever nailed the Weinstein story, so the most important thing was to do it cleanly. Purdy wasn't ignoring the possibility of more severe transgressions; he was saying that if the reporters could break the story, everything was likely to tumble out.

On Saturday, July 15, Jodi checked her phone to find a series of panicked text messages and missed calls from Paltrow. Harvey Weinstein was standing in the living room of Paltrow's Hamptons home. She was hiding in her upstairs bathroom to avoid him.

His timing was the surprise, not his presence. Paltrow had heard from him a week or two before. He had caught wind of a party she was throwing, for potential investors in a musical she was backing, and he asked to come. She felt that he was clearly sending a message—*I'm watching you.* And now he had shown up early, probably trying to speak to her alone, throwing Paltrow off balance. Jodi was anxious too, especially when she saw the accumulation of texts from Paltrow.

From many miles away, Jodi willed Paltrow to stay the course. After the party, Paltrow called: the party had proceeded without incident.

She had kept her assistant close. She sounded undeterred—maybe even a little fascinated by what was unfolding.

On the first Friday in August, Jodi and Megan met Paltrow for the first time at her home in the Hamptons. The hope was to encourage her to go on the record. On a back deck, surrounded by bench swings and lush hedges, the interview began. In person, Paltrow was earthy and funny. She asked Megan empathetic questions about new motherhood before retelling her Weinstein story, and she nodded enthusiastically when Megan carefully pushed for elaboration and told her that the reporters would seek to contact Brad Pitt for confirmation of her account. That was standard procedure, Megan told the star: to corroborate the accounts of alleged victims, they would reach out to people they had told at the time, checking to make sure they remembered the stories the same way.

In the middle of the interview, Paltrow picked up a call from a famous friend, walked out onto the lawn to ask if she had ever been victimized by Weinstein, then returned to explain that the woman had said nothing ever happened. She had not managed to convince other actresses to speak about Weinstein problems. One declined because she was friendly with the producer's wife. Others hadn't gotten back to Paltrow. She wanted to go on the record, but she didn't want the story to be about her. The more women who spoke in the article, the better. "I want to make sure that I'm not in any way at the focal point," she said.

In the car on the way back from the Hamptons, Jodi and Megan were encouraged. Paltrow hadn't said yes, but they had connected in person. Then the reporters realized that they might be able to catch someone who had not answered their inquiries: a former Miramax executive who lived nearby. So they took a detour and pulled up to the woman's summer cottage. She came to the door and greeted them with a smile. But as soon as she understood why they were there, she slammed the door in their faces, leaving them alone on the front porch.

Rebecca Corbett immediately wanted to hear every detail about the Hamptons trip. As an editor, she fully inhabited stories, worrying them forward, living through her reporters while also maintaining a critical eye. Weinstein, who liked to boast of his coziness with media power players, had likely never heard of Corbett. She was sixtysomething, skeptical, scrupulous, and allergic to flashiness or exaggeration, the cohead of the *Times* investigations department but so low profile that she barely surfaced in Google search results. Her ambition was journalistic, not personal.

But she was admired in newspaper circles because of one quality she did share with Weinstein: she had exerted outsized influence by championing other people's work. Like Jodi and Megan, she had come of age in male-dominated newsrooms, raising a daughter in the middle of story sprints. Later, people would say that two women had broken the Weinstein story, but it had really been three.

As Corbett tracked the growing body of hotel room stories, she had one chief concern. "What is your strategy for getting these women on the record?" she asked every few days. Jodi and Megan had a sort-of answer: if we find enough of them, we can urge everyone to go public at once, for safety in numbers.

That was too risky an approach for Corbett. The sources were extremely reluctant, for understandable reasons. There was something inherently unfair in this kind of reporting: Why was it their burden to publicly tell uncomfortable stories when they had never done anything wrong? Corbett was worried that Jodi and Megan could end up with a shocking pile of off-the-record hotel room stories but no article. Even if the reporters did manage to persuade one or two women, that could lead to the old "he said, she said" problem.

The journalists were realizing the Weinstein story would have to be broken with evidence: on-the-record accounts, ideally, but also the overwhelming force of written, legal, and financial proof.

CHAPTER THREE

HOW TO SILENCE A VICTIM

IN MID-JULY, WITH Jodi focused on Hollywood, Megan turned to a basic investigative question: Were there any public records of abusive behavior by Weinstein?

After all, there were laws to protect victims of sexual harassment and, at least in theory, government agencies enforcing them. If Weinstein had been a serial harasser, some of his victims might have filed complaints with the federal Equal Employment Opportunity Commission (EEOC) or the corresponding state agencies in New York and Los Angeles, the cities where Weinstein had run his companies.

The federal and New York agencies had nothing on file. But Grace Ashford, a savvy young researcher in her first month at the *Times*, obtained a report from California's Department of Fair Employment and Housing, which showed several workplace complaints for Miramax. The information was hidden in confusing official government language: addresses, dates, and numerical codes representing the nature of the allegation and how it was resolved, but nothing about who the people were or what had happened to them.

On September 12, 2001, the agency had received a complaint of sexual harassment against Miramax. Strangely, the complaint had been closed the same day. The report suggested that the agency had signed off on the merits of the complaint and steered it into the civil legal system. But there was nothing further, nor was there any record of a court case in California. How could a complaint filed with the government disappear within hours?

Megan kept calling the agency to ask, but it was like ringing a house where no one was home. When she finally reached someone by email, the government official told her the complaint against Miramax and any other related records had been destroyed under an agency policy that got rid of documents in their records after three years. Another policy prohibited the official from providing the name of the person who had filed the allegation.

This was maddening. After some additional questioning, Megan got the name of the government investigator who had been assigned the case at the time that it was filed. The woman was retired. No one at the agency knew where she lived. Through social media sites and address searches, Megan found her living east of Los Angeles and finally got her on the phone.

The interview was brief. The former investigator had reviewed hundreds of complaints during her time with the California agency. She didn't recall this one.

"What's Miramax?" she asked.

On the afternoon of July 14, the *Times* team that had convened to work on harassment stories after the O'Reilly scoop—including Rebecca Corbett, Matt Purdy, Emily Steel, and others—filed into the empty Page

One conference room for an update. The room had no decorations, no pictures of presidents or historic events. But twice a day, top editors gathered at the Page One meeting to debate which stories would lead the print and digital editions of the paper. Reporters almost never attended those meetings, so being there lent this session a heightened quality.

The new harassment stories were promising. Two weeks before, Katie Benner, who covered Silicon Valley, had published a detailed exposé of harassment in the tech industry, about female entrepreneurs who sought funding for their new businesses and were instead harassed by the powerful men who controlled investment money. The story had impact. One of the men and one of the firms had apologized. The women were praised by peers and readers for sharing their experiences. Benner's inbox swelled with new accounts and tips.

That meant the success of the O'Reilly story was no longer a one-off. Megan and Jodi had texted Benner's article, and the supportive reactions, to their Weinstein sources, as if to say *yes, this is tricky, but our team knows how to do it.*

The meeting opened with quick updates: Jodi and Megan were making slow but real progress on Weinstein. Emily Steel was hearing alarming accounts of violations at the media company Vice. Catrin Einhorn was immersed in conversations with restaurant, retail, hotel, and construction workers. Susan Chira was focusing on formerly male-dominated workplaces, like shipyards and coal mines.

In each industry, harassment flourished in its own way. In restaurants, managers didn't want to confront customers who got out of line. Silicon Valley was filled with young men who got rich overnight and felt accountable to no one. In shipyards, construction sites, and other traditionally male workplaces, men sometimes tried to drive out women by putting them in physical danger. Chira had heard of one woman who had been left deep in a mine without any communication device, and another had been stranded atop a wind turbine.

The journalists had come to the project knowing the basics about sexual harassment. Since the 1960s, a body of law had emerged to protect people from unwanted advances in the workplace. Sexual harassment was not a criminal offense, unless it involved rape or assault, but it was a violation of federal civil rights laws, which protected all people's basic freedoms. As the reporters combined what they were learning across industries, they were coming to a deeper realization: some of the weapons intended to fight sexual harassment were actually enabling it.

Emily Steel had the first lead, from her work on Fox and O'Reilly. It was common knowledge that many sexual harassment cases had relied on settlements that imposed confidentiality—essentially paying victims to keep quiet. But the specific terms of the agreements were crying out for further investigation.

From what Steel was learning, the language of the deals made them seem like cover-ups. The agreements included one restrictive clause, or section, after another. The women Steel reported on had to turn over all their evidence—audio recordings, diaries, emails, backup files, any other shred of proof—to O'Reilly and his lawyers. They and in one case their attorneys were not allowed to help any other women who might have similar claims against O'Reilly. If they received subpoenas—court orders—compelling them to talk, they were required to notify O'Reilly and his team, who could fight their being called to testify.

The lawyer for one of the women agreed to switch sides, to "provide legal advice to O'Reilly regarding sexual harassment matters," according to the language of the agreement. Another of the alleged victims promised never to make negative statements about O'Reilly or Fox News, "written or oral, direct or indirect," and not to respond—ever—to any journalists who might contact her about the matter. As part of the deal, she confirmed that she had not filed a complaint with any of the government agencies responsible for fighting sexual harassment, including the EEOC.

In return, one alleged victim received about $9 million, and another got $3.25 million. If either woman violated any of these clauses, she could lose the money. Whatever O'Reilly had or hadn't done to the women was thus dropped down a deep well, never to be recovered. Cash for silence; that was the deal.

That summer, as Steel continued to look into O'Reilly, she also had broader questions: Were these clauses even legal? Were women across the country signing documents like these every day, without anyone knowing? And were sexual harassment lawyers actually tackling the problem they claimed to fight or pumping out settlements for their own profit?

Steel had suggested to editors that the paper delve into those questions, so this was part of the assignment Corbett had given Jodi. In between trying to reach movie stars, she had been calling attorneys and legal experts across the country, from small-town employment lawyers to university scholars, and now she shared her findings.

The kinds of clauses that Steel described were not unusual, the lawyers said. This was standard practice for dealing with sexual harassment, and often one of the only ways of dealing with it at all.

Women signed these agreements for good reason, the attorneys had emphasized. They needed the money, wanted privacy, didn't see better options, or just wanted to move on. They could avoid being branded tattletales, liars, flirts, or hungry to sue. This was a way to get paid and get on with their lives. The alternative, taking this kind of lawsuit to court, was punishing. Federal sexual harassment laws were weak, leaving out many categories of workers. Victims often had as little as six months to file a complaint and, even if they went to court and won their trial, could not get enough money in damages to cover the cost of a good lawyer. No wonder many viewed settlements as surer propositions.

The deals worked out for the lawyers too, especially financially. They generally got paid only if the client did, taking at least one-third of the client's settlement award as a fee. Losing in court could mean getting nothing, so lawyers preferred to reach a settlement—it was sure to pay them something.

Even the EEOC, the government agency that was supposed to enforce sexual harassment laws, often kept its settlements confidential. By law, the agency was required to settle whenever possible, often revealing little information. "We know internally who the companies are that have the most charges," Chai Feldblum, then the commissioner of the EEOC, had told Jodi. But the agency was not allowed to make that information public. Before taking a job, a woman could not check with the EEOC to see what kind of record her potential employer had on harassment. No wonder Megan hadn't gotten anywhere with the old Miramax complaints to the California agency. Such agencies would gather crucial information with taxpayer dollars and then, for the most part, were required to lock it away where almost no one could see it.

Jodi cut to the point: the United States had a system for silencing sexual harassment claims, which often, rather than stopping harassment, made the harassers feel they could do anything they wanted. Women routinely signed away the right to talk about their own experiences. Harassers often continued onward, finding fresh ground on which to commit the same offenses. The settlements and confidentiality agreements were almost never examined in law school classrooms or open court. This was why the public had never really understood that this was happening. Even those in the room with long histories of covering gender issues had never fully registered what was going on.

Leaving the meeting, Jodi and Megan realized how much needed to be investigated. Would the public be interested in these confusing legal issues? There was some reason to be optimistic: after the publication of Benner's story, Benner heard from activists and legislators in California who wanted to change the state's rules on the legality of secret settlements for sexual abuse.

But if Harvey Weinstein had entered into settlements with women besides Rose McGowan, and if those claims had been hushed up by lawyers, could those women even be found?

In 2005, the Weinstein brothers had given up control of Miramax, their first movie company. But many of its former employees remained connected, bound by having together worked through terrible and wonderful moments, sometimes almost simultaneously. For many, working there had been an education, a proving ground, a privilege, and a trauma. You could influence the world's moviegoing taste, negotiate a deal on a yacht in Cannes, and lose every shred of your dignity to the boss's lashings all in the same day.

Every day that July, Megan and Jodi continued to reach out to former employees, one member passing them to the next. The former employees who supposedly knew the most did not return calls; some had been rumored to have assisted with Weinstein's abuses. But the reporters asked other ex-employees for tips: Had anyone heard anything over the years about women accepting settlements?

On the last weekend of July, two weeks after the all-hands-on-deck meeting in the Page One conference room, Megan drove north, away from New York City, through the winding roads of a lush suburb. She was pursuing the mystery of an assistant in Miramax's early years who had abruptly quit.

Megan knew her name. Starting at Miramax, she had impressed others as smart and serious and been quickly promoted. But then, in 1990, she had disappeared, leaving behind only running shoes tucked neatly under her desk. In phone interviews, several former Miramax employees had recalled hearing that Weinstein had done something to her. But no one knew the details.

The most promising clue came from Kathy DeClesis, who had served as an assistant to Bob Weinstein at the time. She said a lawyer for the woman's father had sent a letter to the office shortly after her disappearance. The specific language escaped her, but DeClesis had the impression that the letter had threatened legal action. Her recollection was more than Megan and Jodi had gotten from anyone else. What had the young woman complained about, how had the matter been resolved, and what had happened to her?

The former assistant had left little online trace of who she was or where she had been living the past twenty-seven years. She wasn't on

LinkedIn. She wasn't on Facebook. But Ashford, the researcher at the *Times*, eventually found her on a far-flung corner of the internet, listed in an employee directory in another city. The photo showed no hint of Hollywood or celebrity. Just a regular fortysomething-year-old white woman with shoulder-length hair and a face free of makeup.

Contacting the former assistant was even harder than identifying her had been. Megan left several messages with the front desk of the woman's workplace, explaining that she was a reporter from the *Times* wanting to speak with her, but never heard back. Even talking to the receptionists was tricky, because she wanted to avoid making the woman's colleagues aware of the sensitive nature of her questions. Megan briefly considered flying to the city where she lived but didn't want to scare off the woman.

But there had also been a local address for her mother in that New York suburb. Megan decided to drive there and explain in person why she wanted to learn about the former assistant's experience. If the mother wasn't home, Megan would leave a handwritten letter with her explanation taped to the door. She arrived at the address to find a grand modern house.

Megan had been knocking on doors uninvited as part of her reporting for more than a decade, but it never got easier. It was often necessary in order to get reluctant sources to talk. Over the years plenty of people had welcomed her into their homes, persuaded by the initiative Megan had shown tracking them down. But she had also encountered people who felt violated by her mere presence. As she rapped on the large wooden door, Megan couldn't help but feel like she was intruding into someone's private life.

The person who appeared in the entrance was not the mother but the woman from the picture on the website. Megan was face-to-face with the former assistant.

A young girl was standing by the woman's side, peering out the doorway. Megan introduced herself as a reporter with the *Times*, and a flash of recognition—or perhaps fear—crossed the woman's face. "I can't believe you found me," she said. She and her daughters were back in New York for summer vacation, she explained. Megan had caught them in the middle of a visit with family friends. Reluctant to say too much in front of the other people in the house, Megan asked if the woman would be willing to join her on the front steps for a minute. She agreed.

As they sat side by side, Megan explained that she and Jodi were hard at work on an investigation of Harvey Weinstein. Their reporting had turned up what appeared to be a pattern of predatory behavior. They had reason to believe that Weinstein may have hurt her when she worked at Miramax. Megan wouldn't have gone to such trouble to find her if it wasn't important.

As she spoke, the corners of the woman's mouth turned up ever so slightly. It wasn't a smile, but it was some hint of recognition. "I've been waiting for this knock on my door for twenty-five years," she said. "All I can say is that I had a business dispute with Miramax, the dispute was resolved amicably, and we've agreed not to discuss it."

Megan paused, turning over the lines in her head. Technically, the woman was saying nothing. But there was meaning to her nondisclosure, as if she were working in the blank spaces between the words. She seemed like she might be saying: *Something bad did in fact happen to me years ago, but I must feed you this carefully crafted line.*

This was exactly how a woman who had signed a settlement would answer. There are times in journalism when the right thing to do is turn and walk away, to leave a source alone. But this was not one of them. Megan was determined to keep the woman talking, if only about unrelated things. How old were her daughters? Megan's own daughter was only four months old. The woman was close in age to Megan, with so many similar reference points. The conversation was easy.

After another half hour of chatting, Megan made her pitch. She asked the former assistant to consider contributing to the *Times* investigation. Megan appreciated how risky it was to break a settlement, but, she said, there were ways to bring settlements to light while protecting sources. Her colleagues had done it with payoffs made by Bill O'Reilly. The woman nodded along. She didn't say no. She didn't say yes. Instead she agreed to give Megan something always coveted by journalists: her cell phone number.

But on her drive back to Brooklyn, Megan got a phone call that punctured her optimism. The woman said she had just spoken to her lawyer. He had instructed her not to talk to the *Times*. Megan maintained a positive tone even as her heart sank. She told the woman that her attorney's advice was predictable, but she didn't have to make a final decision yet. All Megan asked was that they stay in touch and continue to discuss options. Reluctantly, the woman agreed.

As she drove, Megan's suspicions were growing. The rumors about the producer had involved actresses, but now she and Jodi were glimpsing an entirely new category of possible victims: employees of Weinstein's companies. The woman who had stood next to Megan on the doorstep—perhaps the patient zero of the Weinstein investigation—wasn't famous at all. And she had been young and vulnerable when she worked at Miramax. Could the producer have abused women more systemically than she or Jodi had ever contemplated? How many women had he victimized since, and would things have been different if the former assistant had been able to speak freely?

On that final weekend of July, Megan still didn't know exactly what had happened to the woman twenty-seven years earlier. But she wanted desperately to keep their conversation going, and so two days after the house visit, she sent the former assistant a text:

> I know I must have thrown you a curveball into your trip home. But please know it's only because this story is so important. There's a real opportunity to make a difference. My hope is that we can continue to be in touch—that I can keep you abreast of what's happening on our end. I suspect you've had some more conversations about this—with family and perhaps others. Seems to me the most important conversation of all is the one you have with yourself.

She also sent a link to the *New York Times* article on O'Reilly's history of settlements. Even as she typed, Megan suspected she might never hear from the woman again.

A few nights later, Megan took another drive, to the home of John Schmidt, a former Miramax executive who had served as the company's chief financial officer in 1990, the year the young assistant had disappeared. Megan figured that Schmidt, who still worked in the film business, would be aware of any settlement the woman might have signed, but he had been dodging her phone calls. So she was staking out his house in Riverdale, a leafy Bronx neighborhood, slouching down every time the local private security patrol drove by, waiting for the living room lights to flick on to indicate that someone was inside. Soon she was face-to-face with Schmidt, apologizing for showing up unannounced at dinnertime, feeling awkward because his wife was also there, listening to her every word.

These settlements were insidious, making victims feel they couldn't speak, potentially saddling them with substantial financial damages if they did, Megan explained to Schmidt. If other people were aware of the payoffs, they were uniquely positioned to provide crucial help. Megan wasn't asking Schmidt to go on the record. She just wanted his perspective on what might have happened all those years ago.

But Schmidt wasn't prepared to speak with her, at least not yet. He told Megan he needed to think about it and escorted her to the door. The reporter understood that people often needed time to come around, but it was frustrating. Some former Weinstein employees appeared aware of problems, and they still wouldn't talk.

One Friday evening that same July, Jodi learned of a respected entertainment executive who had worked at Miramax. Her name was Amy Israel, and she was both wary and bursting to talk.

"I want to have a long career; I don't want to be marked by this," Israel said as soon as she got on the phone. "I do not want to be quoted, period, end of story." But a memory had troubled her for almost twenty years, and she wanted to share it.

In the autumn of 1998, she had attended the Venice Film Festival with Weinstein, scouting for new films to buy. During a meeting in Weinstein's hotel suite, she saw that something appeared visibly wrong with two female assistants, Zelda Perkins, a fixture of the London office, and Rowena Chiu, a more recent hire.

"The two of them were sitting there trembling," Israel recalled. "They were literally vibrating with fear." Weinstein seemed fine, talking about films as usual. Something had just happened involving the two women, Israel had intuited. Weinstein was refusing to acknowledge it.

Israel knew about Weinstein's offenses from firsthand experience. He had praised her, trusted her with significant responsibility at a young age, and harassed her, she said. But all these years later, she feared that what had happened in Venice was worse. She knew only bits of the aftermath. Zelda Perkins had left the company and signed some sort of contract that prevented her from speaking about what had happened—a settlement, Jodi thought. Israel also recommended she call another former employee of the London office, a woman named Laura Madden: she might have something to say too.

Israel was also asking a bigger question: What had all of them, the whole former Miramax crowd, tolerated? That was what she really wanted to know, and the reason she was on the phone with a reporter. Back in the day, Israel had taken small steps to protect colleagues, like forbidding female subordinates from being alone with Weinstein. Doing more had felt impossible—she had only suspicions about what had happened in Venice, and there were few realistic paths to make complaints. When she had reported her own hotel room encounter with Weinstein to one of her supervisors, she was told that another colleague had been victimized too, but no action was taken.

She and her peers focused on their work. "He counted on my shame to keep me silent," she said. "Why are we not speaking out?" Israel said on the phone. "Why are people still not talking twenty years later?"

A few weeks later, on Wednesday, August 9, Jodi was in London, sitting across a restaurant table from Zelda Perkins in South Kensington, hearing her account of what had taken place in 1998.

Perkins had a no-nonsense manner. She worked mostly in theater, a longtime staff member to one of the top stage and screen producers in town, working on major plays and occasionally television series like *The Crown*. She spent time in a cottage in the countryside, where she tended to a flock of sheep, and returned to London frequently for work. Because she was legally prohibited from talking about it, only a small number of people knew the full story of her career.

This meeting was the most Perkins had opened up to any of the journalists who had contacted her over the years about the Weinstein rumors. (The others had all been men, she said pointedly.) With her voice low, she plunged back into the story she had started to tell on the phone, when Jodi had first contacted her.

In 1995, Perkins had ended up working for Weinstein when he was near the peak of his powers. She was only twenty-two years old and had gotten the job through a chance meeting. "I didn't know who he was, and I didn't have a driving ambition to work in the movie industry," she said. She noted that she hadn't been sophisticated enough to understand how prestigious her new job was.

Weinstein had harassed Perkins from practically the first day, and she told Jodi he seemed addicted to conquering women. "That was what got him out of bed in the morning."

Perkins never gave in to Weinstein's advances. She was small but tough, and she had come to the job prepared. Another female colleague had instructed her to sit in armchairs, not sofas, in his presence, so he couldn't sit next to her easily, and to wear her winter parka for protection even if she was warm. "I always managed to say no," she said.

While the hazards of working for Weinstein were beyond anything she had ever seen, so were the perks. On trips to Paris and Rome, "he would just hand out the cash, which was your blood money," she said. "You'd come back from trips with him with a weird comedown of guilt and relief that you'd survived." Each trip felt like a bungee jump, she said, exhilarating but close to the void. Sometimes, he would close the trips on a generous note, saying to Perkins: take the company jet, keep the suite at the fancy hotel for the weekend, invite your boyfriend to come, have fun. "We all took the gifts," she said.

In 1998, Perkins hired another assistant, Rowena Chiu, a creative and driven aspiring producer. Perkins warned her to be careful around the producer. That September, the two women flew to Italy for the Venice Film Festival and the standard Weinstein festival routine: screenings, a stay in a top hotel, and meetings with colleagues from New York, including Amy Israel.

But before the meeting that Israel had remembered, Chiu had come to Perkins for help. When Chiu confided the disturbing details of what Weinstein had done to her the night before, Perkins teared up, said it was unacceptable, and had set off in pursuit of him.

But she couldn't share the details of what Chiu had told her, Perkins said at lunch. Those were for Chiu to describe or keep forever private.

Much later, Chiu told Jodi that part of the story herself. On the Venice trip, it had been her job to tend to Weinstein in the evenings, putting her alone with him in a hotel room for long hours at night. He made advances on her from the beginning, she said, but on the second or third night of the festival, according to Chiu, his behavior worsened. They were supposed to be going through a stack of scripts, and as they paged through, he flattered her, telling her she had real insight and a feel for the business, but he was also relentless, making an escalating series of sexual requests and racial comments while touching her constantly.

"I didn't directly say no; I didn't want to be that confrontational," she said. "He was much bigger than me, and as long as he was being pleasant, I wanted to be pleasant too."

The harassment and groping continued for four hours and kept getting worse, more physically intimate, she said. She dutifully continued on her shift, leaving the hotel room around two a.m., when the work was finally done.

Later, Weinstein denied the whole story. "There is not a bit of truth," he said through a representative, "and any reporting retelling this narrative is just continuing the falsehood."

In London, Perkins went on with her story: She had found Weinstein at a business lunch on the hotel terrace. In front of all the other guests at the table, she commanded him to follow her. He trailed her down the hallway as if she were the boss and he the assistant. When she confronted him, he swore on the life of his wife and children he had done nothing wrong, Perkins remembered.

She was twenty-four years old by then, the older of the two women and the employee of longer standing. Chiu, her assistant, had her account of the incident, but Perkins knew about her boss's record of misbehavior. Chiu and Perkins banded together and resigned. "I had to protect her," Perkins said. "She couldn't have done anything on her own; it would have just been her word against his. I was her shield."

Perkins consulted with a more senior producer who urged Perkins to get a lawyer. She and Chiu, a part-time law student at the time, found a law practice in London and assumed that the next stop would be a criminal trial.

The lawyers told the two women otherwise. They had no physical evidence. They had not called the police in Venice. They were two twentysomethings going up against Weinstein and potentially Disney, which now owned Miramax. Instead they were told that their best course of action was a settlement—maybe a year's salary. This is how such cases were typically handled, they were informed. Perkins and Chiu protested that they did not want any money: it had to be donated to charity, which they hoped would create a public flag. That wasn't how things worked, they were told. Weinstein's attorneys weren't likely to even enter a negotiation without a financial request.

Indignant, Perkins named an even higher figure and then attempted to craft a settlement that would go some way toward stopping Weinstein's behavior. She demanded that Weinstein attend therapy and that she be present for his first session. Miramax would finally have a sexual harassment policy, with training and a group of three people to evaluate complaints, one of whom had to be an attorney. If anyone made a similar allegation in the next two years, with a settlement of at least six months' salary, the matter would be reported to Disney or Weinstein would be dismissed.

Weinstein's lawyers fought back. One negotiating session lasted until five in the morning. In the end, each woman received 125,000 pounds, but both had to agree to extraordinary restrictions.

As Perkins and Jodi ate lunch and talked in London, written proof of those restrictions was sitting in Perkins's bag. Though Jodi and Megan knew about Rose McGowan's settlement, and suspected that one had been struck with the former assistant Megan had met, the reporters had never actually laid eyes on any of the Weinstein settlement papers. In investigative journalism, knowing about incriminating documents was good; seeing them was excellent; and having copies was best. In the days before Jodi's trip, Megan had given her pep talks and sent her encouragement by emoji: *You'll see the papers. I know you will.*

Now Perkins hesitated before drawing the battered sheets with the distinctive old Miramax logo out of her bag. She began to read aloud. She was not permitted to speak to anybody about her time working at Miramax. Any "medical professional" she consulted about what happened would need to sign a confidentiality agreement. She could not be truthful with her own accountant about the money she received. In the agreement, she had to list everyone she had already told about the events in Venice—not by name, Perkins had fought off that part. Instead there was an odd, anonymous list of parties who knew: she told three employees and her boyfriend that she left Miramax "because of an act" and for moral reasons; she told her two closest friends the precise nature of what happened; and so on.

The roll call of restrictions went on. She was not to speak to "any other media now or hereafter existing" about what happened. (*God bless Perkins*, Jodi thought, *sitting here with a reporter almost twenty years later*.) "In the event there is disclosure by the parties," Perkins continued, she would be required to help conceal the truth even if it somehow got out.

These restrictions were insults to common sense. Though the settlement shaped Perkins's life, she wasn't even allowed to hold on to a complete copy of the paperwork. Instead she was allowed limited visitation rights—if she wanted to see it, she could view a copy at her lawyer's office. The papers that Perkins had brought to lunch were just bits and pieces. When she had asked her lawyer how she could possibly abide by an agreement she couldn't consult, the lawyer had given her these excerpts. Worst of all, after intense pressure from the Weinstein lawyers, Perkins and Chiu, who had a matching agreement, had agreed to confidentiality clauses that implied that the two of them could never discuss the matter again.

The date on the documents was October 23, 1998. The mess in Venice had taken just weeks to erase. Chiu sent Perkins a thank-you gift, a calendar planner, then disappeared from her view.

Afterward, Perkins felt "broken and disillusioned." Her search for a new job was uncomfortable because she couldn't explain to prospective employers why she had left a top company so abruptly. Her career in film was over, she realized. She went to Guatemala to train horses. She had fought hard in the settlement negotiations for the right to attend therapy with Weinstein and had chosen a therapist for him, but she had trouble making the sessions happen and gave up.

The 1999 Academy Awards, which took place five months after the papers were signed, belonged to *Shakespeare in Love*. The film won seven Oscars, more than any other movie that year. Gwyneth Paltrow won Best Actress. Weinstein took home Best Picture. Perkins's name was in the end credits for the film.

Over the nearly two decades since, Perkins's perspective had expanded. She was no longer driven, she said, by wanting to get Harvey Weinstein. Perkins wanted to publicly question the fairness of the entire settlement system, to prevent other women from being pressured to sign away their rights.

"For me, the bigger trauma was what had happened with lawyers," she said later. "I wanted Harvey to be exposed, but what broke my heart is what happened when I went to the lawyers."

Perkins was tempted to defy her stifling confidentiality agreement and speak out, and Jodi was impressed by her courage. So many other women would barely get on the phone, and here Perkins was thinking of exposing herself to serious financial and legal risk. Before traveling to London, Jodi had phoned a top employment lawyer there for an assessment of how much a woman with a settlement would risk if she broke the agreement and spoke out. The attorney was clear. "They'll sue her, ask for the money back," he said. In all of his years practicing law, he said, no client had ever breached a confidentiality agreement. "They're paying for silence," he finished. Perkins decided, like everyone else, that she wanted company: if Jodi and Megan could get other women to break their settlement agreements, she would too.

A safer, if less satisfying, way to proceed was to document the basic facts of her settlement by speaking with others. Amy Israel knew a chunk of what happened, and she wasn't the only one. But that still left another problem. Chiu, the alleged victim, was not responding to emails or phone messages. She did not want to be found.

The week before the London trip, Jodi had gotten on an airplane to California, rented a car, and driven up to Chiu's house in Silicon Valley.

Like Megan a few weeks before, she had a note on nice stationery and a mental script.

A man stood in the driveway, fiddling with a car. Jodi introduced herself and asked if Rowena Chiu was home.

No, she was out of the country, he said. But he was her husband, and he was certain that his wife didn't want to speak to any journalists. Could she please leave?

Jodi nodded. Before she went, she asked the husband if they could just speak for a few moments, off the record, right there in the driveway. She wanted to explain why she had come all the way from New York. He didn't say his name, but she already knew it: Andrew Cheung. She tried to read his face. It must have been strange to be cleaning out the car in the driveway one moment, then finding a reporter there the next.

Cheung nodded tentatively. As soon as Jodi laid out the broad strokes, he started asking questions. "You're not the only journalist who has been contacting my wife," he said. "Why are all of these reporters trying to reach her?"

Surely, he knew the answer, Jodi wondered. It seemed impossible that multiple reporters were approaching his wife and he had no idea why. He was probably testing Jodi to see how much she knew and was employing the same script that Megan had heard from the former assistant in the New York suburbs, not even acknowledging that anything happened.

How to respond? She could not lie. She had shown up in this man's driveway asking to speak. If she wanted this couple to be forthcoming with her, she had to be transparent with them too. But at that point, she did not yet know the specifics of the allegations, and if he really had no idea about whatever had happened in Venice, Jodi should not be the one to inform him.

Jodi gently shared that she thought his wife might have been victimized by Harvey Weinstein, making clear that she could be wrong. When she mentioned a settlement, Cheung laughed and gestured at the ordinary-looking house behind him. "Do I look like a man whose wife got a settlement?" he asked.

He really doesn't know, Jodi realized with dread. This woman had never told her own husband. All these years later, the confidentiality clauses had left all three of them in bizarre positions: A woman barred from sharing her own experiences with her spouse. A husband standing incredulously in his own driveway, learning his wife's secrets from a stranger. He promised to relay a message to her but said he was sure that she wanted to be left alone. If Weinstein had victimized so many women, he asked, can't you just do your article and leave her out?

Before she drove away, hoping she hadn't just made things worse, Jodi answered his question. "If everyone takes that stance, the story will never be written," she said.

After she left, Cheung asked his wife, who was then staying with her parents in her native United Kingdom, about Jodi's visit, but Chiu brushed it away, and Cheung didn't want to inquire further. He knew she had worked at Miramax, but because he had no idea about the alleged assault or the settlement, he was also ignorant of one of the most telling details of her employment: nine months after the Venice Film Festival, she had returned to the company.

She hadn't wanted to. But like Perkins, she found interviewing for other film jobs in London hopeless under the unexplainable circumstances. As part of the agreement, Miramax had already given her a reference letter, so she asked the company lawyer for job leads at other organizations.

The message she got back was: Harvey really values you and would like you back.

Chiu caved and returned to Miramax in the summer of 1999, to a job based in Hong Kong, scouting for Asian films that could be made into Hollywood productions. She had no contact with Weinstein, save for one conference call, with a company lawyer on the line to supervise, and wondered what other employees knew—but of course she couldn't ask them.

"I did my best to make a fresh start. It was a whole new country," she said. "I tried to see it as, 'I'm building my own empire and I'm far from New York and the abuse of Miramax headquarters.'" At the start, she threw herself into finding Asian films but found that Miramax was not serious about the material. She slowly began to suspect that the job was designed to keep her under Weinstein's control.

"It was a deal with the devil," she said. She fell into a depression and attempted suicide twice before finally leaving Miramax for good and moving back to London, where she studied for an MBA and began to create a new life for herself.

By the time Jodi showed up in her driveway, she had a résumé full of accomplishment and adventure in the world of business and economics, and four children, including an infant. Chiu told her husband to ignore Jodi's visit. Journalists turned up from time to time, she assured him, but they never wrote anything, and she didn't think they ever would.

Twenty-four hours after the lunch in London with Zelda Perkins, on Thursday, August 3, Jodi was sitting at a picnic table opposite the other woman Amy Israel had recommended: Laura Madden.

When Jodi had asked if she could come see her, Madden had hesitantly said yes. She lived in Wales, but that week she would be on vacation in Cornwall, in the far southwest of England, and she could only spare an hour or so. Jodi went anyway. The flights from London were sold out, so she took a five-hour train ride. In the final hour, the train broke down, so she took a bus. She absolutely had to see Madden, because her story, which she had already started to share haltingly over the phone, brought together so much of what the reporters had already heard.

In 1992, Madden had been just twenty-one or twenty-two, a girl from rural Ireland with little life experience who had grown up feeling isolated on an estate her family had owned for generations. There was no great fortune left—her parents kept the place going as a hotel. As a child, her pleasures were books and roaming the family property, which held farms and gardens. Madden did not attend university, and aside from a few months of language study in Spain, she had never really been away from home.

When a film began shooting nearby, she got a job wrangling extras and caught the movie bug. That crew told her to look for work on *Into the West*, a film starring Gabriel Byrne and Ellen Barkin. She was hired, and that was how she found herself dispatched to Weinstein's hotel room in Dublin one day, excited for the chance to answer calls and run errands for the producer, whom she had never met. When she arrived, champagne and sandwiches were waiting. Weinstein complimented Madden, telling her everyone on the production had noticed her talent and hard work.

"He told me that I was guaranteed a permanent job in the Miramax London office, to start immediately," Madden wrote in an email to Jodi later. "I was delighted, as this was literally my dream job."

On that very day, Weinstein sexually abused her, she said, leaving her sobbing until she could run out of the room. The most painful part was that she had felt so enthusiastic at the start of the assignment, tingling at her opportunity and luck. "The overwhelming feeling I can still remember was shame and disappointment that something so full of promise had become reduced to this," she said. "All the optimism I felt for my future was robbed by him. Any hope that I had been offered a job through my own merit was gone."

Afterward, a female colleague she'd enlisted for support phoned Weinstein to confront him about his behavior, and he readily apologized. "I was to take the job and never feel compromised," Madden said. The producer swore that it would never happen again.

Madden did take the London job, and she spent six years working in production for the man who had abused her, she said. It had seemed safe in part because he was based in the States. The work was what she had wanted, after all. Her father, at first livid at the mistreatment, eventually backed the decision.

But Madden was never happy at Miramax. When the producer visited London, she never knew which version of him she would see: the charming or the dangerous one. She had plenty more uncomfortable moments in hotel rooms with Weinstein, she said, even if none were as bad. She spent the whole of her employment feeling "compromised"—her word—by what had happened at the start. "I carried the weight of feeling responsible for the assault and that I should have outright turned him down and never taken the job," she wrote later.

Madden's story offered clarity, bringing together the elements of what Jodi and Megan were starting to call the Pattern: Weinstein's hallmark moves, so similar from woman to woman. Each of these stories was upsetting unto itself, but even more telling, more chilling, was their uncanny repetition. Actresses and former film company employees, women who did not know one another, who lived in different countries, were telling the reporters variations on the same story, using some of the same words, describing such similar scenes. Eager young women, new recruits to Miramax, hoping to connect with the producer. Hotel suites. Waiting bottles of champagne. Weinstein in a bathrobe. They had been so young, so overpowered. They had all wanted what young Laura Madden had wanted: their own equivalent of that job in the London office, the chance to work, participate, and succeed.

As she and Madden talked, Jodi did not mention the lunch with Perkins the day before, nor had she mentioned Madden to Perkins. She couldn't: the conversations were confidential. Though the two women had worked alongside one another in the London office, they had never shared their painful stories with each other. Both women were isolated; no one could see the whole picture. It was tempting to daydream about bringing all of the alleged Weinstein victims together somehow, to show them that they had each been part of something larger. But that would be dangerous, even with their permission, for the reporters as well as the women. One source could not know who the others were. Anxiety was contagious, the reporters knew. One woman could talk the rest out of participating. One leak could ruin everything.

Earlier, on the phone, Madden had said she would never be able to tell the story publicly. After Miramax she had gone on to experience deep happiness from motherhood. But now she was at a profound point of struggle. Her marriage had just ended. She was figuring out how to be a single mother to her four children, ages eleven to sixteen. She had recently had breast cancer, had lost one breast, and would need a second surgery in the coming months. She'd barely worked full-time since leaving Miramax.

Besides, her feeling of having been somehow at fault had never lifted. She could never speak out, she told Jodi, because she was too afraid of being judged for not running away from her abuser.

But she was speaking privately to Jodi because of a call she had gotten prior to any of their conversations, from an ex-assistant of Weinstein's named Pamela Lubell, to whom she had not spoken in almost two decades. Lubell had gone on about how lucky they had all been to work for Miramax, how kind Weinstein had been. Then she asked if Madden had gotten calls from any journalists—"cockroach journalists," she had said. Lubell had wanted assurances that Madden wouldn't speak to them. Madden had refused to make any promises, so Lubell continued to call and push. "If you ever have a project you want to make, you can bring it to me; I can bring it to Harvey," she remembered Lubell saying. Madden was certain that Weinstein had put her old colleague up to the calls. She was direct with Lubell. Yes, Weinstein had harassed her. No, she could not provide any assurance that she wouldn't speak. In fact, she was outraged by the attempt to silence her. That's why she had taken Jodi's first call.

On the beach, Jodi asked Madden to just imagine going on the record with her story. She sketched out the growing scale of the allegations, without using names; told Madden that her story would mean a great deal to others; and promised to go over everything before publication and do whatever she could to make the experience as dignified as possible. If Weinstein retaliated in any way, that would only seal the case against him, she added.

Madden said, cautiously, that she would think about it. She wanted the story to work. Now that Jodi understood the level of personal difficulty Madden was facing, she worried the timing was just wrong for the former assistant. But privately, Madden was thinking the opposite: "Everything felt like it was imploding," she said. "An added bit of implosion didn't seem like such a bad thing." She was craving something proactive, something positive.

And in her own mind, Madden was formulating an even more potent argument to herself. She realized that she was free. She no longer worked in Hollywood. Even more important, she had neither received money to stay silent nor signed a nondisclosure agreement. She began to wonder if she had a responsibility to speak because others could not.

Back in New York, Megan was making one final effort to track down the mysterious 2001 complaint against Miramax filed at the California Department of Fair Employment and Housing. She needed help from someone who knew the territory, who would understand why Megan didn't want to give up. She sent an email to Gloria Allred.

Megan had become acquainted with the feminist attorney in October 2016 while reporting on Trump's treatment of women. Allred represented several women who had come forward with allegations against Trump. She had put on tightly controlled press conferences, comforting her clients when they teared up in front of the cameras. When Trump lashed out at his accusers, Allred fought back. Some journalists and critics saw her as a shameless self-promoter. But after having read Allred's autobiography, spoken with her at length, and interviewed some of her former clients and co-workers, Megan took her very seriously. She knew that as a young, single parent, Allred had struggled to collect child support, and had been sexually assaulted at age twenty-five. Allred's drive to help protect other women and give voice to victims appeared to be the product of her own suffering.

One thing made Megan cautious about seeking help from Allred on the Weinstein investigation: the strange outreach from Lisa Bloom, Allred's daughter. So when she spoke to Allred, she didn't mention Weinstein's name, only that she needed advice on how to obtain an old sexual harassment complaint from a government agency in her state. Allred was quiet, with little advice to give. Megan didn't realize, and would never have suspected, that Allred's firm was sitting on separate records about Weinstein, ones that had never come to the attention of the government or the public.

While the attorney had built up a reputation for giving female victims a voice, some of her work and her pay were in negotiating secret settlements that silenced them and buried allegations of sexual harassment and assault. In 2011, she and a partner had negotiated a settlement with Bill O'Reilly—one so breathtakingly restrictive that it had alarmed Emily Steel. In late 2016, when the public was first starting to learn about abuse of elite gymnasts by former team doctor Larry Nassar, Allred was working on a settlement that hushed up Olympic-medal-winning gymnast McKayla Maroney, one of the top names in the sport.

Megan only learned months later that in 2004, Allred's firm had also negotiated a settlement with Weinstein. Ashley Matthau (then her last name was Anderson), a dancer in one of his films who said she was assaulted by him, turned to Allred because of her reputation for helping women. Fearful of going up against Weinstein, and all his power, in public, the woman had quickly agreed to accept $125,000 in exchange for a legally binding promise to never speak of the allegations again, she said. Forty percent of the money went to Allred's firm.

In a separate interview, Allred made the same case for confidential settlements that the reporters had already heard: they were better for clients, many of whom wanted privacy and feared being shunned by employers; going to court was risky and could take years. "Nobody has forced anyone to sign an NDA," she told Megan. "Nobody is holding a gun to their head."

Allred also acknowledged the harsh truth about confidentiality clauses: they helped abusers too. "A client will say, 'I want to be compensated. This is a significant amount you've been able to achieve for

me; I'm very happy with that, but why should I have to keep secret?'"
Allred said. "That's because that powerful figure wants peace, wants to
end it, and wants to move on in the same way that you want to move on."

By 2017, a group of consumer lawyers in California, Allred's home
state, had come to see danger in that line of thinking. They thought victims of sexual harassment deserved financial compensation, but settlements shouldn't be used to cover up—and thus perpetuate—predatory
behavior. "If there's a serial perpetrator out there, you can't keep these
secrets repeatedly because the actions will continue," Nancy Peverini,
a lobbyist for the consumer lawyer group, later told Megan.

That January, a California state legislator had considered propos-
ing a law, requested by those lawyers, that would transform settlements
for sexual harassment in California by banning confidentiality clauses
and ensuring that future victims could speak out and name the perpetrators. This was the push that Katie Benner had mentioned to her
Times colleagues in the Page One conference room.

Then Allred stepped in and spoke with an aide in the legislator's
office. Allred was adamant: sexual harassers would never make payments to victims without getting silence in return. If the legislation
was proposed, she would travel to the state capitol to oppose it. No bill
to protect victims could possibly survive public attack from Gloria
Allred. She had many fans who thought of her as the ultimate advocate.
Not surprisingly, the lawmaker backed away from sponsoring the bill.
With Allred's threat, an effort to reform the system and protect victims'
voices died before it was ever introduced.

CHAPTER FOUR

"POSITIVE REPUTATION MANAGEMENT"

ON JULY 12, Dean Baquet, the executive editor of the *Times*, gathered Jodi, Megan, Rebecca Corbett, and Matt Purdy in his office. He wanted to hear about the progress of the Weinstein story. But he also had instructions. Within the newsroom, Baquet's corner office was a place apart, roomier and quieter, containing mementos from a lifetime in the newspaper business. Baquet had grown up in New Orleans, in an apartment behind his parents' Creole restaurant, which was so modest that a cigar box had served as the original cash register. He was the first Black editor of the *Times*, but he rarely opened up to his staff about his personal experience of race. Instead, he liked to talk about holding the powerful to account, when to be aggressive or restrained in dealing with them.

That day, Baquet wanted to communicate one thing in particular: watch out. In 2014, when an early version of Weinstein's troubled theatrical production *Finding Neverland* opened in Cambridge, Massachusetts, Weinstein had tried to get the paper not to review it, knowing that one bad notice could doom the show. He had complained to Baquet and Arthur Sulzberger, then the *Times* publisher, making a not-so-subtle reference to the money he spent on advertising in the paper and citing a tradition of New York publications not reviewing out-of-town tryouts. But one of the culture editors had persuaded Baquet that the rule was outdated: *Finding Neverland* was a big-budget production, and in the online era, the show was no secret.

Baquet was contacted by David Boies, one of the most distinguished lawyers in the country, best known for helping to convince the Supreme Court to overturn California's ban on gay marriage. He had been serving as a legal adviser for the producer since 2001. But when he dialed Baquet in 2014 to argue against reviewing the *Finding Neverland* tryout, Boies had opened by saying: "I'm not calling as Harvey's lawyer; I'm calling as Harvey's friend." The attorney was being insincere about his relationship with Weinstein, Baquet felt, and he had found Boies's chummy I-just-want-to-straighten-things-out-for-you tone condescending. Baquet refused to change his stance.

The following year, *Finding Neverland* was about to make its Broadway debut, and the *Times* was preparing a story on the production. Weinstein yelled at an editor in the *Times* culture department to remove any mention of a glaring development: he had just come under police investigation in New York, for the groping complaint from the Italian model Ambra Battilana Gutierrez. The producer insisted that the accusation was false, and he argued that the *Times* should ignore it, even though it had already gotten widespread coverage in the paper and elsewhere.

Baquet told his staff to keep the reference, and he instructed

Weinstein never to speak to his journalists that way again. "You and I are going to have a pretty rough talk soon about how you talk to my editors," Baquet had written in an email to Weinstein in March 2015. "And it will be very rough, trust me."

An investigation of the producer's treatment of women had far higher stakes than any theater coverage, and Baquet predicted that Weinstein would do just about anything to try to stop it. The editor didn't make a big deal of it, but both Weinstein and Boies had already begun calling him and the publisher, requesting off-the-record conversations.

Baquet wanted Jodi and Megan to follow two rules as they went forward. First, expect Weinstein to turn to increasingly desperate practices: hiring private investigators to follow them or their sources, digging into their pasts. He leveled his gaze at the reporters. "Assume you're being followed," he told them. "Talk like every call is being taped." Second, Baquet did not want the reporters to speak with Weinstein off the record. That would take discipline. What reporter wouldn't want to engage with a subject directly? But Jodi and Megan needed to be strategic, Baquet said. To allow Weinstein to talk in confidence could mean letting him lie with impunity. If he had something to say, he had to say it out loud, on the record.

But in the first week of August, Megan began to question Baquet's rules of engagement after Jodi got an unexpected phone call. It was from Lanny Davis, a Washington lawyer who ran a lucrative business working as a crisis adviser, often representing unsavory characters. He had just been hired by Weinstein and wanted to chat off the record. Jodi told him that all communication had to be on the record, but when he resisted, she took the request to Megan and Corbett. As Jodi waited, Davis kept asking her more questions: Could they meet—immediately? Could David Boies join them? "He is a close friend of the client," Davis emailed, repeating the line that had annoyed Baquet years before.

Jodi and Corbett had dealt with Lanny Davis before. He was old school and outwardly cordial, though he had also been known to yell at reporters he thought were treating him or his clients unfairly.

Despite everything Baquet had said, Megan pushed to meet with Davis. She understood the boss's argument, but in her experience, if you engaged with people who had things to hide, they often hung themselves by accident. Besides, she was curious. How had Weinstein supposedly killed previous investigations by journalists? If the producer was up to something, she wanted to know sooner rather than later.

Megan proposed that she and Jodi talk with Davis on background, meaning they could further report and write about what he said, as long as they didn't attribute any of it to him—his name wouldn't appear in reference to the information. A couple days later, Corbett said that Jodi and Megan could move forward with the meeting with Davis. But she and Baquet stipulated that the session couldn't serve as a substitute for an on-the-record conversation with Weinstein. Boies was not welcome. And while the reporters had to be straightforward, they would reveal nothing of the actresses and former employees who had begun to quietly tell their troubling stories.

As soon as Jodi called Davis to iron out the details, the talkative PR man started spilling information about his client. "He's obviously going through very rocky times," Davis said of Weinstein. "And he's not always that rational."

On August 3, Davis pulled up a seat at a long table in a *Times* conference room, chatting about baseball, being one of Hillary Clinton's closest friends, and his years at Yale Law School. Corbett had joined Jodi and Megan for the meeting, a mark of the seriousness of the moment. Megan took out her iPhone and, with Davis's permission, began audio recording their conversation. As often happened, the click of that button ended the small talk.

"The reason I'm here is not to try to kill anything or not to try to spin or misdirect," Davis said. He had several other goals in mind.

His first goal was to defend. He mentioned the veiled rape claim Rose McGowan had made against Weinstein on Twitter the year before. His team knew she might include the allegation in the memoir she was writing. If Jodi and Megan were intending to report the charge, Davis wanted a chance to respond to the accusation.

That was easy. Of course the *Times* would ask Weinstein to address any allegations—that was the norm for any article. But the investigation wasn't yet at the point of presenting their findings to Weinstein and then evaluating his responses. Today Jodi and Megan were mainly going to listen to what Davis had to say.

His second goal was to probe: "I don't expect you to name sources, especially in a story like this one—but if it's possible for you to let me know overall what your story is about, it would help me basically do my job, which is to answer your questions and make sure they're true," Davis said.

Another simple one. Jodi and Megan told Davis they were looking into problematic behavior toward women by Weinstein and left it at that. Straightforward, without endangering any of their sources.

His third goal was to pitch. While Weinstein adamantly denied any allegation of rape or assault, he was aware of a growing number of complaints about his treatment of women, Davis explained. Weinstein had started to see his previous behavior in a different light. Powerful men of an older generation were changing their understanding of the permission they had when they were with women, of the meaning of the word "consensual," Davis said, and "why women don't feel it's consensual even if a man convinces himself it is."

Where was Davis going with this? Was Weinstein willing to give Megan and Jodi an interview, in which he would discuss his own questionable behavior toward women?

Davis had just started talking to Weinstein about this possibility, he said, noting that his client had to "deal with his wife and children before anything else." But he thought the producer might be willing to have this discussion with the reporters. "I've been at least a little bit encouraged" that it could happen, he said.

This was only the first meeting with Weinstein's team, and his side seemed to already be acknowledging misconduct. That was a hint that the full extent of the findings could be far worse. If Weinstein was already really willing to talk about wrongs he had committed, the interview could be monumental and the investigation much easier than any of them had anticipated. But the idea of Weinstein coming into the newsroom and opening up about sexual misconduct was unlikely. Almost no one ever admitted to these things without being confronted with evidence.

The journalists told Davis that of course they'd be open to hearing anything the producer had to say—on the record. They left it at that: if

Davis was trying to dangle some sort of trade, a halt to their investigation in exchange for an interview, they weren't engaging.

Instead, Megan changed the subject back to Rose McGowan. Davis was adamant that her rape accusation was false and that a main reason she should not be trusted was the absence of any "contemporaneous outcry" at the time of the alleged attack. "Did she tell anybody right away? Did she show signs of distress?" he asked.

But McGowan had told Megan and Jodi that she had indeed appeared upset immediately after her encounter with Weinstein in a hotel room in 1997. She had told her manager, and then a lawyer, who had helped her obtain the $100,000 payment from Weinstein. McGowan had not yet gone on the record with the reporters, and they were still searching for corroboration that she had gotten a settlement. Maybe by pressing Davis on his characterization of events, Megan could back him into a corner and confirm that a settlement had been paid.

Megan leaned in: Was Davis sure McGowan hadn't shown any signs of distress at the time? Was last year's tweet the first time Weinstein had learned of any concerns that the actress had about an encounter with him? Davis's narrative shifted. "Concerns?" he said. "Yes, there—he was aware that there were concerns, but not that she was accusing him of rape. So I'm making a bright line on the word 'rape.' Anything below that line, he was aware of feeling, concerns . . ."

Corbett asked, "Of what kind?"

"And if the concerns were not about rape," Jodi asked, "then what were they about?"

Davis had intended to tell the journalists what Weinstein hadn't done to McGowan. Now he had to explain what the producer had done.

He said that Weinstein was beginning to learn that, because he was in such a powerful position, the women he was with might, after the fact, feel that they were manipulated due to their "unequal position."

Davis added that Lisa Bloom had been working with Weinstein to help him understand his past conduct.

Lisa Bloom! The attorney who had emailed Jodi a few weeks before. What else was there to know about her relationship with the producer? But instead of asking that question, they needed to press Davis on what Weinstein knew about McGowan and when.

If Weinstein had in fact been made aware of McGowan's concerns at the time, how did he respond?

"I believe he had dealings legally with her about them," Davis said.

"How would you characterize those legal dealings?" Megan asked.

They were that close to confirmation of a settlement.

"I think he became aware that she did not regard what happened as okay with her," Davis said. "I'm not talking about rape; I'm talking about the effect that he had on Rose McGowan. She says that it was a severe effect. That rather than fighting . . ."

"Rather than fighting—then what?" Megan asked.

"I think that he has agreed to settlements rather than litigating what he might have litigated," Davis said. As Weinstein saw it, Davis explained, "It's better to settle even if you haven't done anything wrong."

Yes. They had been interacting with Weinstein's side for only minutes, and Davis was already confirming the settlement Weinstein had paid to McGowan and hinting at a larger pattern of payoffs.

Megan asked: Had Weinstein settled with other women as well? The reporters didn't say so, but so far they were aware that settlements had been paid to McGowan, Perkins, and Chiu, and they believed one might have been paid to the assistant who had fled the New York office. Megan had also come to suspect that Ambra Battilana Gutierrez, who made the police complaint in 2015, had been paid off. Did Davis know the truth?

Now Davis, squirming, admitted even more. "The answer is yes, there have been, but I just need to find out how I can better define that for you."

Before he departed, Megan wanted to ask one more thing. Baquet's warnings about private detectives, intimidation, and threats lingered in her mind. She asked the lawyer: Aside from hiring Davis, what else had Weinstein done in response to the interviews she and Jodi were conducting? Had he tried to interfere with the reporting in any way?

"Listen, the guy can be a jerk," Davis said. "Depends on the mood he's in and how much food he's eaten."

But no, he insisted, the producer had no intentions of getting in the way of their reporting. Davis said he had asked Weinstein that question directly during their first meeting: "Do you have any plans to engage people to go on the attack for anyone who's cooperating with the *New York Times*? I need to know."

Davis said Weinstein's answer was unequivocal: "No" and "I don't intend to do that."

Davis left the conference room promising to pursue the potential interview with Weinstein. The journalists were still skeptical but felt encouraged. Perhaps Weinstein recognized that he couldn't halt the *Times* investigation. Just as important, Davis was recorded saying Weinstein wouldn't even try.

But the producer had been ahead of the investigation from the start. His efforts to hide his alleged offenses had begun all the way back in October 2016, when McGowan had first tweeted, *New York* magazine had tried to pursue the story, and Weinstein had told Paltrow not to speak. He had spent hundreds of thousands of dollars to identify people who might talk, to cover his tracks, and even to obtain passages from McGowan's memoir as she was writing it. By the time of Davis's meeting at the *Times*, he had been combating Jodi and Megan's work in ways that went far beyond labeling them "cockroach journalists."

The astounding thing was how much help he had.

On July 10, two days before the meeting in Baquet's office and about a month before the conversation with Lanny Davis, David Boies was preparing to board a private helicopter in the posh village of East Hampton following a family birthday celebration. Weinstein rang his phone— again. The producer had been calling the lawyer frequently, according to Weinstein's assistants.

Cloaked in the secrecy of attorney-client privilege, a rule that protects conversations between a client and lawyer and allows them to remain secret forever, the two men were plotting how to fight any *Times* story.

Weinstein was calling to share a fresh idea, Boies later recalled. The producer explained that he considered Arthur Sulzberger Jr., the *Times* publisher, to be a friend. Weinstein's companies had been a major advertiser over the years. The two men had shared business lunches and long moved in similar circles. Now Weinstein could use that relationship to lean on Sulzberger Jr. to kill the story, he suggested.

The producer and the lawyer, who had been working together for sixteen years, had opposite styles. Weinstein was bold but unpredictable, brutish, and sometimes unsophisticated; Boies was polished and persuasive. The lawyer restrained some of the producer's worst instincts but allowed others to flourish, even though the man he knew had been repeatedly accused of predatory behavior.

The son of teachers from Illinois, Boies had grown up with undiagnosed dyslexia that stunted his learning. Yet he had gone on to earn a law degree from Yale and take on big corporations. Boies was daring and had offended previous law partners with his rebellious ways. He also liked to be at the center of popular culture. Years before he had helped win the fight for gay marriage, he had represented Vice President Al Gore against George W. Bush in the 2000 presidential vote recount.

Among those seeking his services at that time were the editors of Miramax Books, a new publishing imprint that Weinstein and his brother, Bob, had launched. Weinstein convinced Boies to write a book, and in the process secured new high-powered legal representation. Within months of their first lunch meeting in 2001, the lawyer was privately helping the producer fight off a potential article about Rowena Chiu's allegation of sexual assault.

In 2002, the *New Yorker* writer Ken Auletta had heard from a source about the settlements that Weinstein had paid to Zelda Perkins and Chiu—the same ones Jodi and Megan were now piecing together fifteen years later. Auletta had been unable to get Perkins and Chiu to speak with him, but he was still hoping to write about the payoffs and the incident that prompted them.

Auletta, David Remnick, the magazine's editor, another editor, and its lawyer met with Weinstein, his brother, Bob, and David Boies to discuss the matter. At first, Boies appeared to be playing referee. When Weinstein insisted he would go to court to get a ruling banning the magazine from publishing the story, Boies patted Weinstein's arm, saying that there was something called the First Amendment that he couldn't get around. But then Boies turned his attention to the journalists, saying that running the story would be a grave mistake.

Boies later told Megan that he had believed Weinstein's claim that his encounter with Chiu had been consensual and that it was possible that women were lying in order to get money from Weinstein, a point he emphasized in the meeting at the *New Yorker*. In a follow-up session with the *New Yorker* journalists the next day, Bob Weinstein handed over copies of personal checks that he had written to pay off the two women on behalf of his brother: proof, he claimed, that no company money had been used for Weinstein's personal affairs. Without a victim's on-the-record allegation of assault, or any proof of misuse of company funds, Auletta said he and his editors agreed he could not write about the settlements.

By then, Boies had become counsel, or lawyer, to the Weinstein brothers, and he was increasingly entangled in their work. Weinstein and Boies attended film openings, charity events, and political fundraisers together, two celebrities among celebrities. Boies admired that "Harvey's always selling something," and in Weinstein he had a valuable link to the film world. Boies invested in the industry himself, forming a production company, the Boies/Schiller Film Group, in 2012, with one of his law partner's sons. Over the years, Boies and the group did business with The Weinstein Company, and Weinstein provided his lawyer valuable favors, including discussing and securing a role for Boies's daughter, an aspiring actress, in Weinstein's film *Silver Linings Playbook*.

Did these film entanglements with Weinstein explain why Boies had worked to conceal mounting allegations of sexual misconduct against the producer? "Well, it could, you know?" Boies said. "If I'm Harvey's lawyer, I'm going to try to keep things under wraps. That's my job, right?"

Boies said that with or without entanglements, "I am very dedicated to my clients."

In the following years, the lawyer continued learning of other accusers. Time and again, he came to Weinstein's defense and helped him to conceal, spin, and silence. He chose to believe Weinstein's claims that he was guilty only of cheating on his wife, but not committing crimes, not assaulting the women. Even years later, after the scale of Weinstein's alleged offenses was revealed, Boies saw no problem with the lengths he had gone to protect him. "When I look back I don't have any regret that I represented him the way I did," he said.

On a summer evening in 2017, when Weinstein raised the prospect of pressuring Sulzberger, the *Times* publisher, Boies swatted away the idea as a waste of time. Pushing like that might have worked elsewhere, but it would prove worthless at the *Times*.

Instead, Boies was focused on a stealthier way to try to block a *Times* story.

The producer had long relied on private detectives to protect his reputation. Those companies were basically professional watchers:

they observed journalists, wrote reports, sometimes even picked through reporters' garbage. According to the unwritten rules of journalist-subject interactions, using private detectives was a shady practice, but not a surprising or illegal one. As Baquet had said, it was something Jodi and Megan should expect.

But nine months earlier, Weinstein had begun a secret relationship with an Israeli firm of a whole different order: Black Cube. "They r strategists and say your firm have used them," Weinstein emailed to Boies. Black Cube did far more than watch other people. It manipulated them as well, even using an actor who adopted a fake identity in order to dupe unsuspecting targets. Others were former military intelligence experts. At the time of the email, two of its operatives had just been arrested on hacking charges in Romania. Boies's law firm, Boies, Schiller & Flexner, had in fact used Black Cube before, and soon the law firm was making an agreement between Weinstein and the Israeli company. Under the terms of a contract struck that October, Weinstein agreed to pay the professional manipulators $100,000 a month to shield his behavior from scrutiny.

Soon the relationship was in full swing.

Seth Freedman, a British freelance journalist, fed Black Cube information that he was collecting from women who Weinstein feared would go public with damaging information about him. Freedman told the women he was a reporter who had worked for the *Guardian*, sometimes claiming he was writing about life in Hollywood, other times the film industry. Katherine Kendall, an actress, and other women who fielded phone calls from Freedman said they spoke freely, never suspecting he was doing anything aside from straightforward journalism.

Black Cube went to work on Benjamin Wallace, the writer investigating Weinstein's treatment of women for *New York* magazine. Freedman had contacted him offering information of interest but never delivering. Wallace had also been approached by a female Black Cube agent posing as a potential source. When they met, Wallace didn't say much to the woman, who called herself Anna, suspecting she might be working for Weinstein. Eventually, he and his editors decided to suspend the investigation. No one was talking, Wallace later explained; the Weinstein story felt like a dead end.

By May 2017, the same agent was targeting Rose McGowan. This time, the woman called herself Diana Filip and said she was a businesswoman from London. She spoke with a German accent, used a British cell phone number, and offered McGowan $60,000 for a speaking event. Over the next months, they met at least three times in whichever city was convenient for McGowan, conversing for hours about women's issues and the woman's stated desire to invest in McGowan's production company. McGowan read her a passage of her memoir.

"She presented as someone who really cared about women," McGowan later told Megan.

Now, in July 2017, Boies helped renegotiate Weinstein's contract with Black Cube. Its mission became much more explicit: to halt Jodi and Megan's investigation.

Black Cube would "provide intelligence which will help the Client's efforts to completely stop the publication of a new negative article in a leading NY newspaper," along with gathering more information from McGowan's book. The agent "Anna," aka Diana Filip, the woman who had approached McGowan and Wallace, would be on the case full time.

So would a so-called freelance journalist. The contract also promised "avatar operators" to create fake identities on social media, linguists, and "operations experts" to concentrate on "social engineering," all of whom would be advised by former heads of the Israeli intelligence services. If Black Cube was able to stop publication of the article, it would earn a $300,000 bonus. Boies signed the new contract on July 11, weeks before Lanny Davis met with Jodi, Megan, and Corbett at the *Times*.

In dangling the prospect of an interview to the journalists, Davis had never mentioned that at his first meeting with Weinstein a Black Cube agent had been present. He only told Megan that much later, saying that he had not known exactly what the agent was doing for his client.

The same week as the meeting with Davis, Jodi received a series of emails from the same Diana Filip. Jodi had never heard of her, but she said she was from an organization in London and that she was staging a series of events devoted to advancing women in the workplace and wanted her to contribute. Jodi had already brushed off the requests, but in an email the woman was persistent: "As you can probably tell, I am very passionate about this project—in fact, this is very much my own initiative," the note said.

Something about the email seemed slightly off—Jodi couldn't say exactly what. She sent the message to the paper's online security expert, who said the URL looked fine. The website, showing a smiling picture of a woman in a business suit, was a call for gender equality in the corporate sphere. By the standards of corporate feminism, the language on the site was tougher than usual, calling for "progressive activism" and "full transparency" from companies.

Instead of beckoning to Jodi, this warned her off. Her job was to gather information and uncover secrets, not participate in activism. And because *Times* ethics rules prohibited journalists from accepting paid speaking gigs, to protect the paper against attempts at buying influence, she couldn't have accepted the money. Nor did she have time for nice-to-meet-you coffee dates.

A few days later, Filip emailed again. Jodi wrote back tersely to convey her lack of interest: "I am tied up, but good luck w your project."

Later the journalist Ronan Farrow would uncover some of Black Cube's work for Weinstein. Boies said he believed the best way for Weinstein to beat back critical stories about his treatment of women was to provide facts that reinforced his defense, and that he thought Black Cube would gather that information. He said he was unaware of the underhanded tactics the firm used against journalists and regretted not paying closer attention. Remarkably, Boies's firm had facilitated an effort to undermine the *Times* investigation while it was also representing the newspaper in legal cases. Boies insisted this did not constitute a conflict of interest, but the *Times* fired his firm, calling its actions "reprehensible."

But in the summer of 2017, Jodi never guessed that the rah-rah feminist messages she was getting were from an actor-agent hired to sabotage their investigation and undercut victims' stories. Nor did she suspect they were connected in any way to Boies. At Baquet's instructions, she and Megan had rejected the attorney's requests to meet with him. He seemed like a distant suit sitting on the sidelines.

Just as Megan and Jodi were sizing up Weinstein's team, Emily Steel sent over a glowing, newly published profile of Gloria Allred and Lisa Bloom in W magazine. GLORIA ALLRED AND LISA BLOOM ARE THE DEFENDERS OF WOMEN IN 2017 read the headline.

The article described Allred's daughter as her heir and equal, the two standing together at the forefront of civil rights issues, especially "the sexual harassment and assault of women by powerful men." The lawyers posed against the beachscape of Allred's Malibu home, looking more like sisters than parent and child.

Like her mother, Bloom sought out public attention. Over the course of her career, she had appeared as a legal analyst on many networks and even hosted her own show on Court TV. She had her own Los Angeles firm, and she appeared to more or less replicate her mother's model: she cultivated high-profile clients and then, in private, often scored big settlements for them.

So why had Bloom signed on to work with a rumored sexual predator? Was it related to the movie deal, the one Bloom had tweeted about triumphantly a few months before? What motivated her, and how did she operate?

Megan told Jodi and Steel that she had first become suspicious of Bloom in 2016 when the lawyer was part of what appeared to be an elaborate effort to draw media attention to unproven allegations against Donald Trump for her own financial gain. Around the same time, some of Bloom's own clients came to criticize her. One client, Tamara Holder, had felt Bloom pushed her to accept an extremely restrictive but lucrative settlement. Bloom denied ever pressuring her to settle and said she goes over settlement agreements line by line with her clients.

"She did not care about me," Holder later told Megan of Bloom. "She cared about the money."

On Saturday night, August 26, Megan unexpectedly heard a story about Lisa Bloom that began to illustrate the work she was doing for Weinstein.

Megan was meeting someone who she hoped would explain an unusual financial transaction involving Weinstein. It appeared that he funneled money raised for amfAR, a charity to fight the disease AIDS, into the pockets of investors for the musical show *Finding Neverland*.

Megan was meeting Tom Ajamie, a lawyer who had been hired by amfAR to look into the matter. He told Megan how investigating Weinstein was like nothing he had ever been through. The producer had blocked his review of the financial transaction at every turn. David Boies had silenced members of the board with NDAs. Meanwhile, the more Ajamie asked around about Weinstein, the more he heard about allegations of sexual harassment and abuse.

Ajamie was so troubled by the claims that he raised them with Bloom when he met her for a drink in Los Angeles in October 2016. Ajamie had met Bloom once before, was impressed by her feminist credentials, and hoped to forge more of a professional relationship. If she was willing to go after powerful men like Donald Trump, surely she wouldn't be afraid to take on Harvey Weinstein, he reasoned. Maybe she was already working with some of his victims?

Bloom told Ajamie that she had never heard any complaints about Weinstein's treatment of women and asked him to keep her posted, he said. But several months later, things got weird. Bloom accepted Ajamie's offer to stay with him and some friends at a condo he rented in

Park City, Utah, during the January 2017 Sundance Film Festival. After attending a party hosted by Weinstein and Jay-Z, Bloom had returned, saying that Weinstein wanted to meet with Ajamie. Reluctantly, he allowed Bloom to bring him to Weinstein's suite at his hotel for breakfast. One minute, Weinstein was lashing out at Ajamie for digging into his past. Moments later, he was pleading that they work out a deal of some kind. All Ajamie had to do was sign an NDA drawn up by Boies agreeing to keep anything he learned about Weinstein secret. "Let's just be friends," Ajamie recalled Weinstein telling him. "We can do business together."

Ajamie rejected any deal in exchange for his silence, and he left the room convinced that the $600,000 amfAR transaction was the least of what the producer had to hide. Afterward, he recalled, as he and Bloom were leaving, she turned to him. During the meeting, Bloom had presented herself as a neutral party and mostly kept quiet. Now she had some advice.

"You know, I think you really should reconsider your position toward him," she said.

"What do you mean?" Ajamie asked.

"He can really help your career," she replied.

By the time of the Park City trip, Bloom had already been working with the producer for six weeks, at a rate of $895 per hour.

Much later, Bloom said that representing Weinstein in 2017 was a "colossal mistake" that she "deeply regretted." "I was naive to believe he had only used inappropriate language with women, and to think that I could get to the root of the problem in a different way, by encouraging him to apologize, which he did when the story broke," she wrote in an email to Jodi and Megan. "Clearly my approach did not go over at all and I should have known better. Should I have assumed that it could have been a lot worse than what I knew at the time? Yes. That's on me."

But contrary to what she wrote in that email, when Bloom was hired by Weinstein in December 2016, she appeared to know a lot about what she was getting into—and proposed a role for herself that was far darker than just encouraging him to apologize. She laid out that vision in a memo, later obtained by Megan, that she sent to Weinstein and to private investigators he had hired.

Bloom opened the memo by tarring McGowan as "a disturbed pathological liar." "I feel equipped to help you against the Roses of the world, because I have represented so many of them," Bloom wrote. "They start out as impressive, bold women, but the more one presses for evidence, the weaknesses and lies are revealed. She doesn't seem to have much going on these days except her rapidly escalating identity as a feminist warrior, which seems to be entirely based on her online rants. For her to keep her 'RoseArmy' following she must continue ramping up the outrageousness of her diatribes."

The memo continued that McGowan "must be stopped" because she was "dangerous" and proposed a plan of action: offer McGowan an intriguing professional opportunity and at the same time plant articles that paint her as "becoming increasingly unglued, so that when someone Googles her this is what pops up and she is discredited." The letter also suggested threatening McGowan with a lawsuit to prevent her from breaking her settlement with Weinstein and that Bloom and Weinstein do a joint interview in which he'd talk apologetically about his evolution on women's issues. She wrote, "It is so key from a reputation management standpoint to be the first to tell the story. I strongly recommend this. If you agree, I'd like to come out and meet with you to go over the story in some detail, so this is done for maximum effectiveness. You should be the hero of the story, not the villain. This is very doable."

She suggested he start a foundation to promote gender equity in the film industry and also work on his "positive reputation management. I Googled your name, and a few obnoxious articles pop up. I work with the leading reputation management company that can backlink to the positive articles to make a 'firewall' which prevents negative pieces from ranking well on Google." She closed the memo with a suggestion to keep these matters hidden from his employees. "I recommend you set up a secure new email account for emails with this team. We shouldn't be emailing on these sensitive matters to your company email as your IT people and others may have access."

Weinstein initially paid Bloom $50,000. The billing records that followed provided her own private accounting of what she did to help Weinstein.

She collaborated with the Black Cube agent "Anna," aka Diana Filip. She huddled with Weinstein and Boies. She helped orchestrate the collection of information on Rose McGowan, Ambra Battilana Gutierrez, Ashley Judd, and other women who might accuse Weinstein. Bloom worked hand in hand with a private investigator hired by Weinstein who was compiling reports on journalists investigating Weinstein, tracking their social media accounts for clues on who their sources were. Just as Baquet had predicted: Weinstein and his team were watching the reporters, using their every click on social media to try to figure out with whom they were talking.

The reports went on for pages, listing who the journalists followed on Twitter and when they had started following them. Several of Jodi and Megan's most important sources were on the list.

Some assessments turned out to be off-kilter. "It is difficult to predict whether McGowan would grant either Farrow or Kantor an interview," the investigator wrote, after Jodi and Megan had already been in conversation with McGowan for weeks. "It seems unlikely Judd would want to go on the record and rehash the 2015 *Variety* article," she noted. And Weinstein "does not believe Paltrow is a threat."

But other notes were scarily on point. Several of the women were described as potential "adverse sources," including the assistant who had fled Miramax in 1990, the one Megan had found at her mother's home.

"Adverse sources" sounded a lot like another word: "adversaries," enemies. With the help of a large team, Weinstein was waging war.

CHAPTER FIVE

A COMPANY'S COMPLICITY

THROUGHOUT AUGUST AND into September 2017, Jodi and Megan had a growing problem: for all they had learned about Weinstein's alleged mistreatment of women, there was little that could be said in print.

One night, Rebecca Corbett took the reporters to a quiet Midtown Manhattan bar and asked for an update. Jodi and Megan listed what they knew so far. The stars who had told them Weinstein stories. The former employees. The settlements.

Corbett knew exactly what material they had. She was making a point. How many women were on the record? How many settlements had been confirmed? Of the women with firsthand accounts of abuse, only Laura Madden had said yes to going on the record, and her answer was not final. Their evidence of the payoffs was incomplete.

"You do not have a publishable story," Corbett said.

Persuading former Weinstein employees to speak was not getting any easier, particularly when it came to the innermost circle of executives who had served with the producer over the years. Talking was not in their self-interest. Why would they want the world to know that they had risen in their careers by enabling a man who seemed to be a predator? The best shot was to convince them that the *Times* investigation was a way to make up for past wrongs, a safe way to address behavior that, perhaps, had eaten away at them.

At the end of a not particularly useful conversation with one executive, Jodi heard something intriguing. The subject was one of Weinstein's top lieutenants, Irwin Reiter, The Weinstein Company's executive vice president for accounting and financial reporting. Former colleagues had described him as the company's institutional memory: he had done the books for the brothers since 1989. He had been described as a loyalist, gruff, and unlikely to be concerned about his boss's treatment of women. But this executive also said something no one else had mentioned. "Irwin Reiter hates Harvey Weinstein," the source said.

Jodi had been holding on to Reiter's phone number, waiting to call until she had some insight into him. Now that moment had come. When she rang him, he said he didn't want to speak—but before he hung up, he gave her his private email address. Jodi tapped out a note, and he responded a few hours later, writing, "In 2017, things being what they are, I have a healthy respect for reporters. Have a great weekend."

Jodi immediately forwarded Irwin's note to Megan, asking, "What's my line?"

Friday, Sep. 15, 2017, 9:11 PM
To: Irwin Reiter
From: Jodi Kantor

Thank you, that means a lot to me. Carefully

documenting the truth seems more important than
ever. I can swing by your place around 11 a.m. on
Monday to introduce myself. (The phone book says 3
Hebron Drive in East Windsor.) Let me know if there's
a better day or time.

Friday, Sep. 15, 2017, 9:46 PM
To: Jodi Kantor
From: Irwin Reiter

You're a great reporter but you really stink at addresses.
I've never in my life lived in New Jersey. I'm thinking
about all of this. I will let you know on Monday what I've
decided.

To keep the dialogue over email going, Jodi made small talk, with
Megan invisibly reading his responses and advising on Jodi's replies.

Soon Reiter sent instructions: to meet him at nine thirty p.m. at
the bar behind the restaurant Little Park, six blocks from his office at
The Weinstein Company. He set rules for the meeting: he would ask the
questions; he reserved the right to leave after five minutes; he would pay
the check. That was fine. Jodi was surprised at his choice of location,
but she didn't question it. If Reiter wanted to meet under Weinstein's
nose, that's what they would do.

On Monday night, September 18, Jodi walked into the bustling restaurant, glancing around: even if Weinstein wasn't there, she wanted
to make sure she didn't know anyone, lest an acquaintance come over

and interrupt. She continued to an almost hidden space in the back that was sparsely populated: a dim bar that looked like a clubby living room, ideal for private conversations, with plenty of room between one cluster of couches and wing chairs and the next. Where was Reiter? And was he a spy, positioned to find out what the reporter knew?

But the short, fiftysomething man in an armchair in the back seemed too nervous to be a plant, glancing over his shoulders and making dark jokes about evading the goons he was sure Weinstein was employing. A few minutes into the conversation, Reiter was still jumpy, but he didn't ask Jodi many questions, and he didn't seem inclined to leave, so she ventured a few of her own. She wanted to know if he had any of the financial details of some of the long-ago settlements. As she probed him about the past, he looked a little puzzled, or maybe even disappointed. Finally he asked: Why are you asking about ancient history when Weinstein has committed so many more recent offenses against his own employees?

Recent offenses.

Jodi and Megan didn't know about many of those; aside from the 2015 police investigation of Weinstein's behavior, they only had a few unconfirmed tips. When Jodi asked Reiter to say more, he tensed, then started speaking vaguely. He mentioned a young development executive who read scripts and another who had worked at The Weinstein Company while in business school. He used initials: EN, LO, and a scramble of others. He was unwilling to offer more. What he really cared about, he said, was stopping Weinstein from what he had been doing in recent years to young women who worked at the company.

For the next two weeks, Jodi and Reiter met every few nights, always late, almost always at the bar behind Little Park. Jodi and Megan told no one beyond the editors. In emails and texts to one another, the journalists just referred to him as "the source" or "Jodi's guy." The accountant swore that each meeting would be the last. His job was on the line. He spoke in a nervous rush, willing to reveal some things but not others, sometimes refusing to attach names, zigzagging between episodes that sounded central and others that seemed irrelevant or hard to prove. He did not claim to understand everything that had happened at the company, and he wasn't telling the story in order.

In between those interviews, Jodi and Megan worked to decode, track down, and back up what he was saying, by speaking with other former employees, obtaining records, and contacting the women Reiter alluded to. Jodi and Megan were focused on the fundamentals: What had Weinstein done to these young women and what evidence could they find?

But it was also dawning on them that Reiter was providing glimpses of a story that would take much longer to report. During two harrowing years inside The Weinstein Company, 2014 and 2015, the producer's danger to women had become much more visible within the company's top ranks, with problems surfacing with disturbing regularity.

Harvey Weinstein had long enlisted some of the people and practices of his illustrious companies—from lawyers to assistants, contracts to work expenses—to further his abuses or hide them. Some employees knew little or nothing as they worked on movie marketing posters and release dates. But over that two-year period, Reiter, the company's most active board member, and Weinstein's own brother and business

· 108 ·

partner all became increasingly aware of and worried about allegations of sexual harassment and abuse against Weinstein. One by one, they all failed to address the problem, and the producer showed a remarkable ability to create his own reality, to make a series of problems simply disappear.

How could a company become so deeply complicit in abuse?

For a long time, Reiter looked away from his boss's treatment of women. He had started at Miramax on July 15, 1989, thirty years old, a Brooklyn College–trained accountant awed by the daring films Weinstein was releasing, so different from the movies shown at most multiplexes. The next year, he noticed the sudden, mysterious departure of the assistant from the tiny New York office—the same woman Megan later approached at her mother's house. He was told that Weinstein had acted inappropriately with her, she had negotiated some sort of settlement, and that was that.

Almost a decade later, Reiter heard Zelda Perkins had a problem in the London office and knew a company lawyer was dispatched to England to help dispose of it. And like many colleagues, Reiter heard rumors of "affairs" between the producer and actresses but felt unsure about who was taking advantage of whom: Weren't actresses known for doing anything for a part? Besides, he was the back-office numbers guy, paid to do the books, without the authority to question Weinstein. He didn't inquire further.

Until 2014, when he became more alarmed. He wasn't yet grappling with whether women had been hurt or how. He was anxious about the state of The Weinstein Company, which projected an image of success but was less stable than outsiders knew, with many failed projects and hundreds of millions of dollars in losses. A sex abuse scandal could send it on a path to destruction.

In November 2014, Reiter composed an accusatory email to Weinstein, naming some of the women he had heard about through the office grapevine. Weeks later, in December 2014, Reiter arrived at work one morning to find some other executives nervous and concerned. A twenty-five-year-old woman named Emily Nestor, a graduate student, had taken a temporary job as a receptionist in the Los Angeles office, filling in during the holiday period. By her second day of work, Weinstein had badgered her into breakfast at the Peninsula Hotel in Beverly Hills and had offered to exchange sex for mentorship, boasting of all the actresses who had supposedly accepted and gone on to fame and fortune. Nestor kept saying no. He kept offering. When she finally got out of there and returned to the office, she told other employees about what had happened, and they alerted their counterparts in New York.

Reiter was worried: the company was facing what sounded like an episode of sexual harassment. Nestor didn't want to file a complaint with the company's human resources department. So Reiter and several other executives persuaded the employees in Los Angeles who had heard her account firsthand to write everything down. One record noted how long it had taken her to fend off Weinstein: "She said he was very persistent and focused though she kept saying no for over an hour."

In early 2015, Reiter sat in a Midtown restaurant arguing with his daughter Shari, who was twenty-six, about the same age as Nestor, a psychology student and a firm feminist. When her father told her what was happening in his workplace, even passing his phone across the dinner table to show her and a law student friend some of the emails and documents, she was appalled. Shari urged her father to act, both recalled later, and she told him he had to find a way to stop Harvey Weinstein's behavior. Reiter wanted to. He was no longer just afraid for the company: he was starting to fear for the safety of female employees and was troubled by the idea of the boss hurting women who worked for him. But he didn't see what could be done. The company's outside lawyers had advised the executives that because Nestor did not want to file an official complaint, sharing her account with the company's board might not make sense. Pushing further felt futile. Besides, he added to his daughter, they both knew what happened in these situations: victims often ended up being blamed, as if they had done something wrong.

Shari pressed forward anyway. The conversation grew heated enough to attract glances from other diners, she remembered later. He had power, she told her father. He could help create an environment where women felt comfortable coming forward, and he was obligated to do more.

That winter, Reiter heard concerns from another young female employee. Sandeep Rehal was Weinstein's personal assistant, twenty-eight years old, working in her first professional job. She began to confide in Reiter and a few other executives about duties she found uncomfortable. Weinstein had ordered her to rent him a furnished apartment, using his corporate credit card to stock it with women's undergarments, flowers, and two bathrobes. She had to maintain a roster of women, which she referred to by a phrase Reiter had heard around the office before: "Friends of Harvey." Managing their comings and goings had somehow become part of her job. For these and other disturbing duties Weinstein gave Rehal a $500 bonus, paid for by the company, according to an email she saw him send to human resources. He had implied there would be consequences if she told anyone about what she was doing for him, mentioning her student loans and where her younger sister attended school, and saying he could have her kicked out. Staying silent would come with rewards, he suggested. "You are at Harvey Weinstein University, and I decide if you graduate," he told her, she said. Soon Rehal left the company, and Reiter did not hear from her again.

But the accountant began complaining more to colleagues about another issue Rehal had raised—use of company expenses. Weinstein charged massive amounts to his company credit card, relying on a loose system to classify which personal expenses he would reimburse. On top of his generous salary—$2.5 million in 2015—he sometimes demanded the film company pick up questionable bills, including a $24,000 tip for yacht staff—which he eventually reimbursed—and a private jet stop in Europe to pick up a model. (Weinstein denied that he ever misused company funds.)

In between Jodi's late-night discussions with Reiter, the reporters continued to scramble to confirm what the accountant was saying. Emily Nestor did not wish to comment publicly about what had happened. But soon Megan was on the phone with another young assistant, whose initials Reiter had provided, who had left The Weinstein Company in the summer of 2015. The woman's voice was shaky. But slowly, she started to explain that she had left the company "for moral reasons." Because she had signed a nondisclosure agreement, she was afraid to tell Megan everything she had experienced. Weinstein had preyed on her, bombarding her with requests for sex and massages that she repeatedly refused. She hadn't wanted to miss the opportunity to be part of such a highly regarded company, so she had worked her way into a new position that provided more distance from him.

When Weinstein demanded that she work for him directly again, she complained to a top executive about meetings with women she was forced to arrange for Weinstein, hoping the executive would help keep her out of the boss's reach, she said. Instead, Weinstein himself called her, pressuring her to deny her allegation, submit a letter saying she had a "positive experience" with the company, and exit.

At the same time, Jodi was having eerily similar conversations with a former assistant named Michelle Franklin, who had worked in the London office in 2012. She was also very anxious about speaking and wanted to talk only off the record. Weinstein had never pressured Franklin for sex. But like the young assistant to whom Megan had spoken, she said she had to arrange hotel room encounters for "Friends of Harvey"—the same term Reiter and others had used, and had responsibilities similar to Rehal. All of these conversations were off the record, but added to the body of knowledge the reporters were accumulating. The similarity of all of their experiences made them even more powerful. (Weinstein denied their accounts.)

One day, as she walked a young woman to Mr. Weinstein's hotel room, Franklin confronted him. "It's not my job, and I don't want to do it," she remembered saying. "Your opinion doesn't count," she said he responded. Soon afterward, she was fired.

On the afternoon of September 19, Megan got her own firsthand experience in Weinstein's ability to exert pressure, enlist others, and shamelessly pretend that problems did not exist.

For two weeks, she had been piecing together more details of how the $600,000 raised at the 2015 AIDS charity auction had instead, through a series of complicated transactions, landed in the account of investors in Weinstein's *Finding Neverland* production. Jodi and the editors were worried that she was pursuing a distraction from the larger target of how Weinstein treated women.

But Megan couldn't let go. She had confirmed that the New York State Attorney General's Office, the state's top prosecutor, was investigating. She had obtained internal records showing that people inside amfAR had expressed grave concerns. In an email, the chief financial officer had written, "Nothing about this deal feels right to me." Legal experts were telling Megan the arrangement might amount to fraud. Even if he hadn't broken the law, Weinstein appeared to have redirected more than half a million dollars for AIDS research to reimburse his own investors.

The story, Megan believed, would show how Weinstein could bend an institution to his will. The producer had maintained a cozy relationship with amfAR for years, helping the organization throw its star-studded fundraiser in Cannes, France—the one with the splashy red-carpet photos Jodi had studied months earlier. David Boies had helped Weinstein silence amfAR's board when it sought an outside investigation. In a recent interview, Boies had walked Megan in a verbal circle for nearly two hours, with Lanny Davis and Charlie Prince, a Weinstein Company attorney, reinforcing the there's-nothing-to-see-here defense.

Now Weinstein himself had arrived at the fourth floor of the *Times* building, determined to face off against Megan and beat back the story.

The interview had been approved by Corbett and Baquet under two conditions: first that it was on the record, and second that it focused solely on the financial transaction, not the allegations about mistreatment of women. Megan was eager to push for answers but also to size up the man she and Jodi had been reporting on for months. Corbett would participate in the meeting to help keep it on track.

The producer wore rumpled clothes and walked with a slight limp. He growled hello, his voice low and nasal with an old-school New York accent. Behind him trailed a posse. Megan wasn't surprised to see Davis and Prince. Another attorney, Jason Lilien, who had apparently just been hired by Weinstein, introduced himself as former head of the Charities Bureau for the New York State Office of the Attorney General. "I know this sounds self-serving, but I quite literally wrote the law in New York on these areas," he told Megan.

The presence of two other members of the group was baffling. Megan shook hands with Roberta Kaplan, the attorney who had successfully argued *United States v. Windsor*, the landmark Supreme Court case that had paved the way to federal gay marriage. Then Megan recognized a tall, striking middle-aged woman with dark hair and a strangely familiar face. She was Karen Duffy, aka "Duff," an MTV video jockey of her youth. Why had they chosen to be by Weinstein's side in a matter that they surely knew nothing about?

Corbett wanted to set the expectations clearly: the meeting was to stay tightly focused on the amfAR transaction.

But Weinstein, it became clear, intended to produce his own narrative. About his awakening to the heartbreak of AIDS, his extensive philanthropic giving, and his concern for the suffering of others. The visitors now seated around the conference room were his supporting players.

At first Weinstein's tone was friendly, if condescending. He began with a tutorial of how the world of charitable fundraising really worked. If the journalists dug deeper, he explained, they would see that creative transactions like the one involving amfAR were extremely common. Everyone did them. You had to run charities like a business if you wanted to do good in the world, he said, pointing out that other money that he helped raise at the auction did go to amfAR.

"And legal schmegal," he said, spreading a smile around the room. "Our idea was to get people help."

It was time to discuss how much he had done to battle AIDS. He recalled first seeing the ravages of the disease close-up when the Broadway director Michael Bennett, of *A Chorus Line* fame, became ill decades ago.

"One day I get a phone call from his person saying that Michael's got pneumonia. And I . . ." Weinstein paused, as if to steady himself. "Okay, all right. I'm gonna get through this," he said.

Soon Weinstein was reading from an actual script, a written statement from a former vice president of amfAR who could not attend the meeting. Using the third person, he described his own compassion and generosity: "Harvey came forward and said: 'Do you need help?'" Weinstein said.

"We did, and he literally took over the auction, badgering people." He appeared to choke up and struggle to get the words out. "I'm not acting," the producer said.

He started again, stopped, as if he was overcome by emotion, and then slid the script over the table to Duffy, who read the rest. With tears in her eyes, she said that Weinstein had helped save her life when she was diagnosed with a rare disease. Now, she said, it was important "to represent the people who really can't talk right now," AIDS victims who had benefited directly from Weinstein's generosity.

Megan let them finish, then launched into more questions. Shouldn't people bidding on items at a charitable auction know where their money was going? Was it appropriate for charitable contributions to ultimately flow back to Weinstein and other *Finding Neverland* investors?

With each round, Weinstein became visibly annoyed. He swung from attacking the paper to expressing his devotion. "I love the *New York Times*," he said. "My famous story is 1977, I'm in this snowstorm in Buffalo, New York, as a student, you know, a guy goes out, it's my friend Gary, 'What are you gonna get at the store?' He says, 'I'm gonna get Twinkies.' The other guy is gonna get milk, the girl says 'I want Cheerios,' whatever. And my famous—and this is a longtime quote, you can probably look it up. I said: 'Just get me the last copy of the *New York Times*.'"

If there was anything untoward about the $600,000 transaction, he insisted, Megan should be pressing the lawyers who were responsible for it. And if the bidders of the auction hadn't figured out that their money was serving his business deal, well, that was their problem. "You don't want to make a donation to that, don't," he said.

Kaplan said that she served on the board of another AIDS charity and suggested that if the *Times* followed through with this story, it could hurt AIDS patients around the world. She did not appear to understand the underlying financial transaction that she had come, in effect, to defend.

Megan asked: Would Weinstein do this type of financial arrangement again?

"Not with you around," the producer joked.

"I think we need to wind this up," Corbett said.

But Weinstein had one last point: he wasn't just fighting for good; he was battling villains. The charity board members who had reported him to the attorney general just wanted to take over the organization to serve their own dark interests.

The Weinstein Company attorney tried to cut in, but Weinstein swatted him away.

"I'd rather go down with the truth," Weinstein told the journalists. "That's what I grew up with. I grew up with the truth."

Megan thanked the group for their time. For all of the theatrics, she was still going to write her story about the $600,000 transaction. She watched the producer leave, trailed by his supporters, and was struck by the display of this man forcing his way through the world, expecting everyone to fall in line.

When Jodi saw the group filtering out, she went down to the lobby. She had made a point of introducing herself to Weinstein before the meeting started, and as he left, she wanted to see him once more, to remind him of Lanny Davis's suggestion of a possible interview.

The producer was standing outside the security turnstiles, amid the usual mix of office workers and tourists snapping pictures of the *Times* sign. When she approached him, he leaned in to Jodi with such intensity that she had to remind herself not to show any signs of intimidation. She told him that while that day's meeting had been about amfAR, she and Megan hoped to interview him later about his treatment of women.

Weinstein started mocking that investigation to his group, describing the findings even though the reporters had never shared them. "Luring them to hotel rooms," he said dismissively.

Let's sit down and talk about it now, he suddenly proposed. "I'll tell you everything. We'll be transparent and there will be no article," he said. "Go ahead, let's do it."

Jodi declined. She and Megan would reach out when they were ready, she said.

He stepped in closer, and Jodi let out a nervous laugh. He hadn't done the terrible things that women were accusing him of, he said. He wasn't that bad.

He smiled mockingly, then said: "I'm worse."

The tactics Weinstein used during the in-person interview over the amfAR transactions were a guide to how he operated. Later, they helped Megan figure out what had happened at his company in March 2015, when the next and most perilous complaint landed, from Ambra Battilana Gutierrez, the Italian model. Emily Nestor and Sandeep Rehal had just left, but this allegation caused far more concern than the others, because for the first time ever, a woman made an accusation against Weinstein in full public view. After going to Weinstein's office for a work meeting, Gutierrez went to the New York Police Department and accused the producer of groping her. The news made headlines at the same time as the company was poised to sell its TV division in a $400 million deal that would have served as a potential lifeline. Reiter, who said he had been promised a million-dollar bonus from the sale, was appalled—this was just what he had feared, a public mess.

The police helped Gutierrez secretly record Weinstein discussing the incident and later said they had been eager to see him charged with sexual abuse.

But the district attorney's office soon announced through a spokesperson that it would not prosecute, saying only that "after analyzing the available evidence, including multiple interviews with both parties, a criminal charge is not supported." Gutierrez left New York without giving interviews or otherwise publicly discussing her complaint against Weinstein, making Reiter and others wonder what had happened behind the scenes.

What almost no one knew at the time was that Weinstein had conducted an elaborate campaign to make the model's allegation disappear.

The criminal lawyer Elkan Abramowitz, a former partner of District Attorney Cy Vance, was the public face of Weinstein's legal team.

Privately, Linda Fairstein, the famed former Manhattan sex crimes prosecutor, provided help too. She was in touch with Weinstein's office about the case and helped connect Weinstein's legal team and the lead prosecutor. (During the summer of 2017, when she had insisted to Megan that the model's allegation was unfounded, Fairstein had not disclosed her ties to the case. Fairstein said later that it was Megan's fault for not asking and that there was nothing unusual about her actions.)

Weinstein's private investigators went to work collecting records on Gutierrez that painted her as a liar. New York prosecutors would later acknowledge they worried she might not seem credible to a jury during a trial given the history that Weinstein had highlighted on her.

Rudolph Giuliani, the former New York mayor, had fielded one of

Weinstein's first phone calls following the police complaint and steered him to a partner in his firm who ended up acting as Gutierrez's lawyer. After prosecutors declined to press charges, Weinstein paid Gutierrez a seven-figure settlement in exchange for her silence and secured Gutierrez's copy of the audio recording she had made of him at the direction of the police.

To the company's leadership and others, Weinstein insisted the entire episode was an elaborate effort to blackmail him—that Gutierrez threatened *him* unless he paid her—but never revealed that he had paid Gutierrez a hefty financial settlement.

"She's a shakedown artist," Lance Maerov, a member of the board, recalled Weinstein telling him. "And, if you don't believe me, I'll have Rudy Giuliani sit down with you."

In a final stroke, Weinstein drew on the power and resources of his own company to help seal his secret deal to silence his accuser. On Saturday evening, April 18, 2015, the producer summoned two of his prominent female executives to a meeting at Giuliani's firm. Gutierrez was present, along with her lawyer. At the producer's instruction, the two women walked the model through steps she could take to break into acting and boost her public profile, people who attended the meeting later recalled.

This was part of the deal both sides had struck: Weinstein would quietly arrange for career assistance for Gutierrez. For the model, it was a way of picking herself up and moving on. For the producer, it was a familiar form of leverage: if you stay quiet, my people and I will help you succeed.

That evening, Weinstein wrote the two executives an email of thanks, which Megan later obtained. It promised each of them a $10,000 bonus.

No one had more incentive to hold Weinstein accountable for his behavior than Bob Weinstein, his brother and long-term business partner.

The brothers had risen in the movie business by relying on a bond that dated back to the childhood bedroom they shared growing up in a modest apartment in Queens. From the age of ten or twelve, Weinstein had been a voracious reader, tracker of talent, and celebrity maven, noting who was on the late-night shows, in the gossip columns and the hot nightclubs. Bob was more inclined toward numbers, later remembering how the family had to stretch when its rent was raised from $86 to $92 a month.

When they launched Miramax, Weinstein commandeered the high-profile movies, while Bob ran the financial modeling and built a lucrative business in horror movies and other mass-market franchises. In those early days of the company, the brothers often stayed on the phone with each other all evening, from nine or ten until one or two in the morning. Some people found Bob difficult to work with in his own right. He was socially awkward and could be kind one moment, then lash out the next. In his older brother, Bob found inspiration, creativity, and drive, comparing their relationship to a marriage, to the "ultimate friendship," to one long, rolling conversation, he said in a series of interviews with Megan.

But The Weinstein Company, founded in 2005, never reached Miramax's cultural or financial heights, and the brothers soon fought about money, Bob's more disciplined approach versus Weinstein's limitless appetite to buy and approve films, rack up massive expenses, then buy and do more. Bob watched with concern as his brother grew obsessed with personal fame, eventually turning himself into a single name: Harvey.

He had also seen evidence of the threat his brother posed to women. Bob had participated in discussions about the confidential settlement that was paid to the young assistant who fled Miramax in 1990, two people familiar with the agreement would later tell Megan, though he denied any knowledge. When Harvey Weinstein needed money to pay off Zelda Perkins and Rowena, Bob wrote the checks. (He later said his brother told him the money was to cover up cheating on his wife.)

But Bob regarded his brother's sexual behavior as just one more form of excess, he told Megan. In his eyes, his brother was "crazy, out of control."

One day in 2010 or 2011, the brothers were arguing about finances in a little room near Weinstein's office. As Bob rose to leave, Weinstein punched him in the face. Several other senior executives were right there, including Reiter. Everyone watched as blood gushed down Bob's face. No one, not even Bob, did anything to hold his brother accountable for the violence.

By that time, even though they shared responsibility for their company, their employees, and the huge sums that had been invested in their business, Bob had decided that he was not his brother's keeper.

From then onward, Bob distanced himself from his brother. They technically co-ran the company, and the world still saw them as a team, but they communicated less and less. The bosses had already been working out of separate buildings. Now the distance took on more meaning.

Bob periodically considered splitting the company in two. Whenever Bob raised the suggestion, his brother would reply: "Sure, we can split the company. I'll get everything, and you'll get nothing." Ultimately, Bob was unwilling to walk away.

Due to his own struggles with alcoholism and his treatment through Alcoholics Anonymous and Al-Anon, Bob convinced himself that his brother's problem was sex addiction, and that no one could stop Harvey Weinstein other than Harvey Weinstein. It was a convenient, and arguably disastrous, moral choice, by which Bob justified his failure to do more. He stayed in business with his brother but excused himself from intervening in his brother's actions. He refused to take responsibility or even help employees who came to him upset about his brother's viciousness.

"People would come into my office and say, 'Your brother's screaming and yelling at me,'" he said. "I said, 'Quit. You're talented.'"

That was what passed for his management style. "Send a note to HR," he would sometimes say to his employees, even though the human resources operation at the company was weak and offered few solutions. "Write a letter."

But in the weeks after the public accusation from Gutierrez, Bob finally felt compelled to act. The $400 million deal to sell the television division was now dead, a major business blow. He feared that without intervention, his brother could do something else even more destructive to the company. Thanks to an accident of timing, he thought he had just the right opening: the employment contracts for the Weinstein brothers and other top executives were expiring at the end of 2015 and there would be negotiations for their renewal, which would involve a review of job performance and discussions of pay and responsibilities. Bob would seize the chance to ensure his brother underwent in-depth professional treatment for his sexual behavior.

That summer, Bob sent David Boies an email containing a letter for his brother. In the email, later obtained by Megan, he expressed his sorrow and anger about years of Weinstein's bullying and other "misbehavior," calling his brother "an empty soul," and conveying his hope that his brother would get professional help to change his ways.

In the letter, Bob made a veiled reference to what happened years earlier at the Venice Film Festival with Perkins and Chiu. He wrote,

> Over the past 15 to twenty years I have been personally involved with the repercussions of your behavior. The reason I state that is for u to truly see how long this has been going on and how it has only gotten worse over time. . . .
>
> There have been instances of behavior that I and David Boies have had to assist u with in getting out of trouble. I am referring to a situation in England. In that case and every and I mean every time u have always minimized your behavior, or misbehavior, and always denigrated the other parties involved in some way as to deflect the fact of your own misdeeds. This always made me, sad and angry that u could or would not acknowledge your own part.

As the letter continued, he wrote about Weinstein's abuses of power:

You have picked on people and used your power over them. You have brought shame to the family and to your company through your misbehavior. . . .

Your reaction was once more to blame the victims, or to minimize the misbehavior in various ways. If u think nothing is wrong with your misbehavior so in this area then announce it to your wife and family.

He sent off the email with an expectation that Weinstein and Boies would come back to him with a plan of action. He signed the letter, "Love Brother, Bob."

At the same time, another company leader separately felt motivated to act. The Weinstein brothers had packed the company's board with allies. A board oversees the performance of a company and helps steer it. The current board members were all male, and most of the seats were taken by wealthy executives from the finance and entertainment industries who took a hands-off approach.

But Lance Maerov, who had been appointed in 2013, was different: his role was watchdog. Maerov represented the interests of major investors in the company who wanted to keep an eye on the brothers. "Just make sure to keep these guys honest," Maerov told Megan later. "That's what my mandate was."

At first he had given little thought to Weinstein's treatment of women. He had heard rumors about the producer putting "friends" in his films, and Weinstein seemed to always have a young woman on his arm at movie screenings and other events, but Maerov believed it was extramarital cheating, nothing more. His focus was sniffing out financial misconduct and trying to address the broader toxicity at the company. "You would walk out of a board meeting and it felt like the most dysfunctional Thanksgiving dinner you've ever sat at," he said of the verbal brawls that erupted between the Weinstein brothers.

But when the groping accusation made headlines, Maerov, like Bob, feared that Weinstein might be engaged in a pattern of sexual behavior that could hurt the company, and wanted to use the contract renewal to force the issue. He and Bob weren't acting as a team; Bob saw Maerov as a threat to his own power. But Maerov was one of the board members in charge of renewing the contracts. In the process, he could take the routine step of examining Weinstein's personnel file, the file the company's human resources department held that would contain any complaints against him or legal actions taken on his behalf.

Weinstein refused to let Maerov see the file, with David Boies backing him up. Boies countered that he would review the file himself and report to the board about any potential legal problems for the company.

Maerov found the proposal ludicrous and was growing distrustful of Boies. Sometimes Boies said he worked for the company, other times for Weinstein, creating what felt like a conflict of interest when it came to potentially damaging information that Weinstein might want to hide from the board.

On the morning of July 1, 2015, Maerov received a secret peek inside the file anyway, thanks to someone who was trying to aid his efforts: Irwin Reiter. The accountant and two other executives sat him down for breakfast at the Four Seasons Hotel in Beverly Hills and began to outline complaints of verbal abuse that had been made against Weinstein over the years. Then Reiter showed Maerov several pieces of paper, Maerov later recalled. It was the memo outlining what Weinstein had done to Emily Nestor, evidence of the exact type of behavior that Maerov suspected.

For Maerov, attempting to scrutinize Weinstein was like nothing that he had experienced in decades of corporate life. Weinstein and Boies worked together, alternating the producer's brute pressure with the attorney's artful persuasion. Maerov said that at a movie premiere during the summer of contract negotiations, Weinstein threatened to punch him. When Maerov complained, Boies responded in a letter, calling the claims "exaggerated," "a bit hysterical," and proof "that anyone who feels as you do about Harvey should not be in a position of trying to negotiate with him." Boies threw Maerov what looked like a bone on the personnel file: Rodgin Cohen, one of the most prominent corporate lawyers in the country, reviewed the file and reported back that nothing in it "could result in liability to the company," meaning that the company couldn't be sued over anything in the file. (What Maerov only learned afterward was that Cohen's son was a junior employee of The Weinstein Company, seeking to get his start in the film business.)

Maerov, Reiter, and Bob Weinstein all felt the situation could not stand. But four months later, in October 2015, Harvey Weinstein signed a brand-new contract that secured his power for years to come. With David Boies's assistance, Weinstein had misled, soothed, and otherwise outmaneuvered Maerov, Reiter, and his own brother.

Maerov also brushed aside key information. When Boies acknowledged to him that Weinstein had paid settlements to women over the years, emphasizing that no company money had been used, Maerov didn't press for details. He also chose to disregard the memo about Emily Nestor he had seen.

He considered the matter taken care of, because in the contract negotiations, Weinstein had agreed to a concession. The company would put a new code of conduct in place, which would require Weinstein to pay hundreds of thousands of dollars in penalties if he entered any new settlements. The contract specified that Weinstein could also be fired for misconduct. It almost read as if the company expected Weinstein to keep accumulating allegations and that the financial penalties could take care of the problem.

Maerov was trying to make sure that if anything went wrong, the company wouldn't suffer. That was different than trying to guarantee that women would not be harassed or hurt. Once Maerov felt assured that the organization was legally protected, and with some additional financial controls in place, he decided he had done enough. Irwin Reiter didn't know what more to do. He had plotted with Bob Weinstein on ways to separate his brother from the company only to watch Bob lose his nerve. He had slipped documents to a board member, but that had no impact. He was only working three days a week, and that summer, the company tried to bring him back full time, at double his salary, for a total of $650,000 a year. He refused. He was more deeply worried than ever: "There is almost no deal I wouldn't sign if HW wasn't my boss and there is no deal I would sign if he is," he wrote to a board member in the summer of 2015. But he remained at the company, working at essentially the same job he had held since he was thirty years old.

Bob Weinstein, who held the most responsibility, walked away satisfied, because his brother finally gave him what he wanted: a promise to stick with intensive therapy for sex addiction, a promise that was impossible to enforce.

"There were many emails where he'd swear that he would do it, and he's going, and he always delayed it, which has led me to go, addict, addict, addict, addict, addict," Bob said.

"You start to hear this, you get worn down—you get worn down. They come at you hard with their lying, just nonstop. I got worn out. I said, 'I surrender,' see?"

Late on the evening of September 28, 2017, five days after Megan's article about the amfAR mess was published, Jodi again met Reiter at the bar behind Little Park. As the employees at The Weinstein Company had read and discussed the article, Reiter had texted Jodi, narrating the reaction from inside the company. He had not been involved in the questionable transactions with the AIDS charity, since Weinstein's theater business was separate. But he and other employees were riveted by the article, he said: they were finally watching someone hold his boss to account. (Weinstein continued to deny wrongdoing, but later, the authorities took action: federal investigators in Manhattan opened a criminal inquiry into the transactions but have made no public comment about where their examination stands. The New York Attorney General's Office wrote a letter to amfAR, saying the transactions raised several concerns, including whether they "resulted in benefits to private interests," and told the charity to strengthen its corporate governance.)

Reiter had already been so helpful, and back at the paper, the editors were already urging Jodi and Megan to start composing a first article about Weinstein. But the reporters wanted more—in particular, more documentation of what had happened at The Weinstein Company during those tumultuous two years, which could be published without anyone fingering the source. Reiter had mentioned a memo written by a well-respected junior executive named Lauren O'Connor, who he said had departed over Weinstein's treatment of women.

Without giving too much away, Jodi wanted to show Reiter that his mounting outrage since 2014 had been justified. A few minutes into the conversation, Jodi reached into her bag, drew out a printout she had prepared a few hours before, and passed it to Reiter. For all his knowledge about what happened inside the company, he knew very little about what had transpired between Weinstein and actresses in hotel rooms. Jodi explained that this was an account she had heard from a well-known actress. The text was just one paragraph, with no names other than Weinstein's, no location or time. It described how the woman had arrived, unsuspecting, to a meeting at a hotel with Weinstein, and to her surprise, been shown upstairs instead. When she got there, he was waiting in a bathrobe and asked for a massage. He tried to pressure her into sex by saying he could help her career. She fled.

As Jodi had guessed, Reiter appeared aghast. She told him that this actress was far from alone, that she and Megan had heard variations on this same narrative again and again, which closely matched the accounts by employees that had already been disturbing him. She and Megan didn't know how many women had these kinds of stories about Weinstein, she said, but based on what they were hearing, the number might be very high.

Jodi asked him again for the O'Connor memo. He had already read her a few quotes, which she had jotted down, but she wanted to understand the document better. Could he pull it up again on his phone? He started to read the memo aloud, then paused.

"I'm going to pay a visit to the little boys' room," he said. He tossed Jodi his phone, open to the email with the memo, rose from the table, and left her alone.

After all of his indignation, his fruitless attempts to intervene, and the moments when he had thrown up his hands, the accountant was finally doing something irreversible to stop his boss.

The first time Reiter had seen the memo had felt like a case of déjà vu. In November 2015, shortly after Weinstein's new contract had been signed, he had arrived at work to find colleagues huddled in an office, once again examining a complaint about Weinstein. This one was from a woman they knew and trusted: O'Connor was an up-and-comer at the company, respected for her taste and work ethic. Unlike Nestor, she had filed a long, detailed complaint, and it went far beyond one incident. Weinstein had said offensive things to her, but she was painting a much broader portrait of how he treated women and how that behavior corrupted the company.

Reiter and the others informed Bob Weinstein, who read the document and agreed that the board needed to know about these accusations. Instead of forwarding the document—too risky—Bob dictated a memo inviting the board members to come to the office to read it in person, waiting half an hour before informing his brother what he had done.

After months of frustration, Reiter felt new hope. The next day at the office, he watched with satisfaction as Maerov sat at a table, looking over the memo. Maerov took photos of the first and last pages, noting all the witnesses and other details that O'Connor had included. "It felt very credible," Maerov said later.

But after that, O'Connor's complaint evaporated, just like the Gutierrez accusation. Reiter couldn't explain it. He figured that Bob Weinstein had lost his nerve yet again. He assumed that David Boies had stepped in to cover his client's misdeeds once more. Soon O'Connor was on her way out the door with little explanation.

Except the allegations had not disappeared: Reiter had seen the memo, and so had several other colleagues. Right after he read it, he stashed away a copy for himself. Nearly two years later, Jodi was sitting blocks away from The Weinstein Company offices with the document in her lap and her source on a very deliberate trip to the bathroom. *He's telling me, without telling me, to copy the memo,* Jodi thought.

She worked quickly, not pausing to read the document, willing her fingers not to make a mistake. After a few clicks, the full memo was in her possession.

When Reiter returned to the table, his phone was waiting on his chair, and Jodi thanked him but didn't overdo it.

As soon as he left, a few minutes later, she headed for the bathroom to send the screenshots to Megan and Corbett. She didn't want sole electronic possession for one more second than necessary. In the subject line of the email, Jodi just wrote "Memo."

Lauren O'Connor had sent the document on Tuesday, November 3, 2015, with an ordinary subject line ("For your records") and introduction: "As requested, I took some time to catalog and summarize . . ." Then she cut to the heart of the matter.

There is a toxic environment for women at this company. I have wanted nothing more than to work hard and succeed here. My reward for my dedication and hard work has been to experience repeated harassment and abuse from the head of this company. I have also been witness to and heard about other verbal and physical assaults Harvey has inflicted on other employees. I am a 28 year old woman trying to make a living and a career. Harvey Weinstein is a 64 year old, world famous man and this is his company. The balance of power is me: 0, Harvey Weinstein: 10.

I am a professional and have tried to be professional. I am not treated that way however. Instead, I am sexualized and diminished. I am young and just starting out in my career, and have been and remain fearful about speaking up. But remaining silent and continuing to be subject to his outrageous behavior is causing me great distress.

The rest of the memo was a detailed portrait of Weinstein's behavior, including an assistant's confession to O'Connor: Weinstein had forced the assistant to give him a massage. "It was horrible to see her so upset," O'Connor wrote. "I would have liked to report this but she asked me to keep it confidential as she feared the repercussions of complaining."

O'Connor detailed Weinstein's advances on women and said that he acknowledged such behavior, but tried to shush her with muddled logic: "We don't talk about it—can I trust you? I mean, I'm a bad boy but what's important is that I'm honest about it."

When O'Connor complained about Weinstein's verbal abuse toward her to a Weinstein Company human resources executive, "the response was basically—let us know if he hits you or crosses a line physically," she wrote.

Her most fundamental complaint was that her job had been turned upside down by Weinstein's upsetting sexual behavior. She had joined The Weinstein Company to turn books into enthralling films, so how had she ended up entangled in her boss's questionable sexual activities?

> On other trips with Harvey, I was instructed by him
> to meet with aspiring actresses after they have had
> a "personal" appointment in Harvey's hotel room.
> Harvey instructed me to greet them when they came
> down to the hotel lobby and facilitate introductions for
> them to managers, and agents, as well as assisting in
> casting them in Weinstein Company projects. Notably,
> only female executives are put in these positions with
> actresses with whom Harvey has a "personal friendship,"
> which to my understanding means he has either had
> or wants to have sexual relations with them. Female
> Weinstein employees are essentially used to facilitate his
> sexual conquests of vulnerable women who hope he will
> get them work.
>
> I am a literary scout and production executive. I was
> hired to find books The Weinstein Company could make

into films, and my role expanded to handle production. Clearly, managing Harvey's past and present sexual conquests was never something I imagined being part of my job responsibilities.

Late that night, when Jodi, Megan, and Corbett read the memo in full, the moral stakes of the investigation suddenly transformed and expanded. What had once been a story about past misdeeds suddenly seemed a far more urgent pursuit. No one had ever stopped this man. If the reporters failed to publish their findings, he might go on to hurt someone else.

CHAPTER SIX

"WHO ELSE IS ON THE RECORD?"

Friday, September 29, 2017

BY MORNING, CORBETT had already shared the memo with Baquet and Purdy. The secret document, from inside the company, which confirmed and detailed the pattern the reporters had been piecing together for months, was crucial. They were looking at the situation from the outside. O'Connor had seen it from the inside. Her memo was like a key turning in a lock.

Corbett, Purdy, and Baquet gave the same instruction: write!

But the team debated what to write. Baquet and Purdy, with the O'Reilly article fresh on their minds, were pushing for a narrower story documenting the settlement trail, which they hoped to get into the paper as quickly as possible. They wanted to lay down a marker, because in recent days, Jodi and Megan had begun to hear footsteps from Ronan Farrow, the reporter who was contacting their sources and had apparently taken his findings to the *New Yorker*. The *Times* team had little sense of his material or how close he was to publication.

Jodi, Megan, and Corbett shared the desire to break the story, but they also knew the material better than Baquet and Purdy. They believed the first article had to be broader and capture the power of what they had heard and documented. The sickening repetition of the hotel room stories. The apparent targeting of women who were new on the job. The terrible bargain of sex for work, and the longstanding silence of those who knew. Corbett pushed the reporters to write the story that the three women were beginning to see in their heads as fast as possible, while trying to hold back Baquet and Purdy.

That story would need names, dates, legal and financial information, on-the-record interviews, and documents. Jodi and Megan pushed aside the half-verified accounts and rumors they were still chasing and made a list of the material that could potentially be solidified enough to be included in a first article, with allegations of harassment and assault marked in black and settlements in red:

1990—Assistant at Miramax, New York. Settlement.

1992—Laura Madden, Ireland.

1994 or '95—Gwyneth Paltrow, Los Angeles.

1996—Ashley Judd, Los Angeles.

1997—Rose McGowan, Park City, Utah. Settlement.

1998—Zelda Perkins and Rowena Chiu, Venice, Italy. Settlement.

2014—Emily Nestor, Los Angeles.

2015—Ambra Battilana Gutierrez, New York. Settlement.

2015—Lauren O'Connor, New York. Settlement?

2015—Assistant in NY leaves for "moral reasons."

A few days before, Lanny Davis had finally given Megan an answer, on background, about how many payoffs Weinstein had made to women:

eight to twelve settlements. Megan paused, somewhat shocked that Weinstein's team would reveal such damning information.

"Do you think that's normal for men to make so many payoffs?" she had asked Davis. "I do," he had replied, in a matter-of-fact tone.

But they still needed a second source to corroborate those figures— because the reporters didn't have written records or other definitive proof, they needed more support. They also needed to contact everyone who might go on the record, including former Miramax and Weinstein Company employees who could attest to the findings. Everyone the reporters planned on mentioning would have to be offered a chance to comment. Now was also the time for them to let O'Connor know that they had a copy of her memo.

The draft would be a work in progress, nearly every line requiring negotiation, fact-checking, adjustment, or deletion.

By Friday afternoon, Corbett, Jodi, and Megan were on a conference call with O'Connor and her attorney, Nicole Page.

Page did most of the talking. O'Connor didn't speak, but it was clear she was distressed that the *Times* had her memo and planned to publish part of it. She had never wanted to go public. She had tried to move on after the debacle of the Weinstein job, with a fresh start at a new company.

She was afraid that Weinstein would retaliate, and Page asked the journalists to reconsider using the memo, or at least to omit O'Connor's name, describing the stress the article would place on her. The journalists exchanged worried glances. The last thing they wanted to do was cause O'Connor trouble. She was young, not yet thirty. And she had spoken up for others who she believed had been victimized, becoming one of the rare figures in the entire Weinstein saga who had dared to raise questions formally about his conduct.

But newsworthy documents are rarely withheld from readers in newspaper reporting. O'Connor wasn't a source who had confided to the reporters with a promise of anonymity; she was the author of a critical indictment of Weinstein that had been circulated at the highest levels of his company and then covered up. Many publications omit the names of sexual assault victims at their request because of the uniquely private nature of that crime. But O'Connor's situation was different: although she described verbally abusive treatment from Weinstein, the power of her memo came from her role as a witness, documenting sexual misconduct by Weinstein toward other women.

Corbett assumed control of the call. Her style was always to hear people out as neutrally as possible, and like Baquet, Corbett usually left reporters to deal with sources. But now she spoke for the institution in a way the reporters could not. The paper had to publish the memo, she said gently but firmly. No, not the whole thing. Yes, they could point out that O'Connor had declined to comment, to try to make clear that she was not the source of the memo, and to spare her from retaliation. Yes, the paper intended to name her as the author of the memo to establish its credibility. Corbett added that if Page or O'Connor wanted to make a further case for leaving her name out, they should.

Page did not respond, and her client remained silent. Page said later that the paper's decision sounded set in stone. The attorney ended the conversation saying she appreciated what the journalists were trying to do. Megan had suspected the reason why O'Connor had not talked during the phone discussion, and with a few more calls she confirmed it: O'Connor had accepted a settlement too. She was legally prohibited from speaking.

Much later, Megan learned the backstory. Right after O'Connor had sent the memo, she was told not to come into the office. Within days, Page was negotiating a settlement with Boies and a Weinstein Company attorney. Boies said he helped craft a cover story for O'Connor: she would stay at the company a few more weeks to finish projects, working in locations that allowed her to avoid any contact with Weinstein. But her career there was over. In an interview with Megan, O'Connor later explained that the company's response to her complaint was: "How can we quickly make this go away?"

Six days after she had sent the memo, the exit agreement had been finalized, Boies said. As required, O'Connor had written a letter to Weinstein thanking him for the opportunity to learn about the entertainment industry, as well as this follow-up note to HR:

> Monday, Nov. 09, 2015, 3:23 PM
> From: O'Connor, Lauren
> Subject: For your records
>
> Because this matter has been resolved and no further action is required, I withdraw my complaint.
>
> Lauren

Jodi and Megan agreed the next move was to contact Lance Maerov, the Weinstein Company board member. In that first story, they wanted to be able to demonstrate what they had started to learn from Reiter about the company's complicity.

Maerov answered the call to his cell phone as he was walking into his Park Avenue office building with a cup of coffee. Megan introduced herself and explained that the *Times* was preparing to publish a story about allegations against Weinstein stretching back decades. She read an excerpt from the O'Connor memo, then asked: "What did you do about it?" The cup slipped from Maerov's hands, spilling scalding coffee. *How in the world does she have those records?* he later recalled thinking.

Only hours afterward, Megan was meeting Maerov in Bryant Park in Midtown Manhattan. Maerov, with his carefully parted hair and expensive scarf, looked every bit the polished businessman.

Maerov explained that, yes, he had been concerned about Weinstein's treatment of women, especially after the NYPD investigation. He told Megan about how Weinstein had called it attempted extortion—blackmail—and the board had approved a code of conduct designed to limit misbehavior. When the board was notified later that year about the O'Connor memo, he said, he wanted an outside lawyer to investigate. But within a day or two, Boies had informed him that the matter was resolved. "Boies told me the complaint was withdrawn," Maerov told Megan. So Maerov had let it go.

Megan nodded as he talked, pressing for more details. She suspected he wasn't telling her everything he knew, but what Maerov was saying was already valuable, especially if she could get it on the record. The Weinstein Company board had in fact been aware of claims of sexual misconduct against Weinstein and, aside from a written code of conduct, had basically looked the other way.

Maerov agreed to be quoted, but he told Megan that he had a duty to tell the other board members that the *Times* story was coming and that he had talked to her. She asked him to please keep quiet over the weekend. Once Weinstein found out they were close to publishing their article, he would intensify his efforts to stop it. She and Jodi needed more time. Maerov agreed to give them two days.

Even though he was somewhat skeptical of the accusations by actresses, Maerov felt some relief as he walked out of the park, he told Megan later. For years, he had mostly failed to hold Weinstein accountable. No matter what surfaced, Weinstein always wiggled out of trouble. Finally someone was closing in.

But Maerov, as usual, felt duty bound to protect The Weinstein Company. Back at his desk, he immediately broke his promise to Megan. He called Bob Weinstein and David Glasser, the company's president, and relayed everything she had told him.

Saturday, September 30, 2017

By that morning, Weinstein somehow knew the details too and called Maerov, begging him to help kill the story: "Lance, I know we have had our differences over the years, but can you just circle the wagons once on my behalf?" Maerov found the conversation so offensive that he took notes.

When Maerov balked, Weinstein tried threatening him, but Maerov was unmoved. His job was to safeguard the company, not the producer. The next day, he emailed Weinstein a single sentence: "We need to discuss a plan to protect TWC in the event that Megan Twohey runs her article."

Meanwhile, Jodi and Megan were at their keyboards, writing. Jodi typed:

> Actors and former assistants told the *NY Times* variations on the same story, in some cases without any knowledge that others had experienced the same.
>
> Because he usually worked out of his [London] hotel room, rarely coming into the office, the women were often alone with him and there was little escape.
>
> Along the way, he enforced a strict code of silence, threatening women who complained, locking employees in nondisclosure agreements.

Megan wove in what they knew of the remarkable events that unfolded in 2015. Gutierrez's police report had never been made public, but a source had read every word to a *Times* colleague over the phone. Now Megan drew on that language to describe how at the work meeting, Weinstein had allegedly grabbed her breasts and put his hands up her skirt. It had never been reported before that behind the scenes, Weinstein had quietly "made a payment" to silence Gutierrez. When O'Connor's memo hit, "with page after page of detailed allegations," Maerov wanted to investigate, but then Weinstein reached a settlement with O'Connor as well.

By Saturday night, they had something resembling a draft to show Corbett. She created a secret file in the *Times* editing system, which only the reporters and relevant editors could open. Typically, stories were labeled, or "slugged," by topic along with dates of when they would be published, for example, 16TRUMPSPEECH, 07EARTHQUAKE, 21BEYONCE. Corbett slugged this one with the generic label 00INQUIRY, so that even colleagues who happened to scroll past the slug in the editing system could not know what the story was about.

Even as the reporters wrote, they were verifying—and trying to expand—exactly what they could say about which alleged offenses, with which sourcing. Jodi and Megan had only one interview with an alleged Weinstein victim on the record: Laura Madden, with her account of her first meeting with him in Dublin in 1992. Because Zelda Perkins was still locked into her confidentiality agreement and Rowena Chiu had not spoken at all, their entire saga shrank down to four short but crucial paragraphs, meant to show that there had been serious allegations and a settlement while still protecting the two women involved.

The assistant from 1990, the one Megan had found at her mother's house, was essential to the story.

In the end, John Schmidt, the former Miramax executive to whom Megan had made an unannounced visit earlier in the summer, confirmed on background that the former assistant had been paid a settlement following a troubling episode with Weinstein. He had agreed to speak with Megan, explaining that he had been impressed by her amfAR article. Megan had not abandoned hope that the woman would go on the record. But when she had reached out to her, this was the response:

Dear Megan,

I'm sorry but please do not try to contact me again,

directly or indirectly. I have nothing to say, nor do I give anyone else authority to speak on my behalf. I do not want to be named or cited as an anonymous source in any article and I will take legal action if this happens.

Because her story seemed to involve a sexual assault, Jodi and Megan would not use her name without permission. They decided to simply refer to her as a young woman who left the company abruptly after an encounter with Weinstein, according to several former employees, and who later received a settlement. They quoted her old boss, Kathy DeClesis, who said: "It wasn't a secret to the inner circle."

Later, Megan would learn that the assistant had allegedly been sexually assaulted by Weinstein when she ran an errand at his home, and Schmidt would tell Megan more: that Weinstein had confessed to him shortly after the encounter that he had done "something terrible." "I don't know what got into me. It won't happen again," Schmidt later recalled Weinstein telling him. (Weinstein denied saying this.)

Next, Megan called Rose McGowan, who had appeared determined to expose Weinstein. But McGowan said she was not in a position to go on the record with her allegations against the producer. Because of a host of complications, she was going to sit this story out. "I'm sorry," McGowan said. "I just can't."

But at Jodi and Megan's urging, McGowan had obtained a copy of the settlement she struck with Weinstein in 1997. Remarkably, the one-page document did not include a confidentiality clause. McGowan was able to share it with the reporters without facing potential legal or financial consequences. McGowan declined to comment for the story, but their article could quote from the document, saying that following an episode in a hotel room during the Sundance Film Festival, Weinstein had paid McGowan $100,000. The payment was "not to be construed as an admission" by Weinstein but intended to avoid a lawsuit "and buy peace."

Most of the former Weinstein employees whom the reporters wanted to quote were scared, fearing retaliation. Jodi and Megan argued that the story would include overwhelming evidence, that even after all these years, it wasn't too late to speak up. Most of them refused. ("I have a life!" protested one executive.) Another offered a quote, but a few hours later, his employer, a major corporation, nixed it, saying it didn't want to be associated with the article.

One of the few who came through was Mark Gill, the former president of Miramax Los Angeles. "From the outside, it seemed golden—the Oscars, the success, the remarkable cultural impact, but behind the scenes, it was a mess, and this was the biggest mess of all," he said, describing the producer's alleged offenses against women. Jodi and Megan counted his line, and a few others, as victories and inserted them into the draft.

At midday on Monday, Jodi texted Ashley Judd, asking if she could speak. Baquet and Purdy were still urging the reporters not to get hung up on the actresses. The crucial task, they said, was to break the story, and after that, they predicted, everything would spill out. It would be fine to get Judd and Paltrow on the record then.

Jodi and Megan disagreed. The Weinstein story had two strands: the producer's apparent menacing of generations of his own employees as well as of actresses who wanted parts. The reporters had the first strand well documented. Without the second—many actresses, even some top stars, said they had been harassed by Weinstein—the story would be incomplete.

Judd texted right back. Yes, she was in a dentist's waiting room and could talk.

For more than three months, Jodi had been laying the groundwork for this moment. Two weeks before, she had met Judd in person. On a terrace high above Manhattan's East Side, Jodi asked her to imagine what going on the record would look like and stressed that she was working to get testimonies from other actresses as well. Judd had listened carefully and said she wasn't sure.

Now the ask felt wrong. The story would be published just before the season premiere of Judd's television series *Berlin Station*, a scenario that she had wanted to avoid. Worse, all Judd had wanted from the beginning was the company of other actresses. But even after dozens of conversations, those accounts had not materialized. Salma Hayek, Uma Thurman, and Angelina Jolie had not gotten on the phone. Jodi was still coaxing Gwyneth Paltrow, but she remained a question mark. Other actresses, prominent and unknown, had told the reporters Weinstein stories and sworn them to secrecy. The pattern that had protected Weinstein for decades—no actress wanted to be the one to speak up and name Weinstein—still held.

On the phone with Judd, Jodi didn't beg or tell Judd how badly she yearned for the actress to go on the record. That could make her sound weak, even desperate, and she wanted Judd to feel confident, in capable hands. She tried to show Judd how strong the article would be: twenty-five years of allegations, a clear pattern, names and examples, human resources records, legal and financial information, and quotes from male and female employees characterizing the problem.

Even as Jodi spoke, she braced for rejection. Judd didn't show her hand.

She promised to take the request seriously and call back soon.

A few hours later, a text from Laura Madden popped up. Jodi had been worrying about losing Madden. The sped-up timeline for the article had created an uncomfortable conflict: Madden's long-dreaded next round of surgery related to her breast cancer was scheduled for October 10. Jodi couldn't give Madden a firm publication date, and it looked like the operation and publication could collide. That was too much stress for any one person to take—but for the journalists, losing Madden would be a disaster.

But instead Madden was worried about being the only woman from the London office on the record. If so, she was out. She asked Jodi more questions about the article: How many women, how many women from this place, this office, this year?

Everyone wanted company, and understandably so.

Monday, October 2, 2017

Just after noon, the reporters filed into Dean Baquet's office to discuss the final step of the investigation: when to take the findings to Weinstein and how much time to give him to respond. After protecting the sources for so long, it was time to approach Weinstein and his representatives, describe the story, and share every allegation they planned to make public. Every anecdote, every date, every woman's name. (They would not mention Judd or Paltrow, who were maybes to go on the record.)

Then Jodi and Megan would incorporate his answers into the article. If he denied the accusations, they would say so. If he apologized, they would print that, in his own words. If he refused to comment, they'd go with that. And if he could disprove any of the allegations, those claims would have to be omitted. For example, if he could prove that he had not been in the same city as a woman alleging abuse, Jodi and Megan would not be able to publish that accusation.

Presenting findings was standard journalistic practice, the right way to treat any story subject, even a completely untrustworthy one. But the group could not settle on how much time to give Weinstein to respond. They would need to provide him with a deadline: here's how long you have until we publish. But once Weinstein knew what the *Times* planned to publish, he could pressure women into taking back their stories, intimidate others into contradicting their accounts, or try to undermine the accusers. He could leak information to another outlet, to reduce the story's impact, or undercut publication by rushing out some sort of statement of apology. The journalists had to protect the victims—and the article.

Six people, all with some form of authority and some final responsibility for guiding the Weinstein story safely into the paper, sat in Baquet's office. Baquet was the boss, the journalist charged with supervising the entire, encyclopedic newspaper every day. The ultimate calls were always his. But Corbett had guided the project from the beginning, and Baquet relied on her in part because her instincts were a little different. They were in running conversation with Matt Purdy, who amid the tumult of supervising many stories across the newsroom was still keeping close watch on the investigation.

But Jodi and Megan as reporters had their own form of authority and responsibility. They had gathered the information. They had the relationships with the sources. They were writing the story, their names would appear at the top in the byline, and they would take a great deal of the blame or credit for whatever happened.

The sixth figure in the room was David McCraw, the *Times* attorney. He was there to keep the paper out of legal trouble, so no one present wanted to reject his advice.

Corbett felt they needed to give Weinstein forty-eight hours, as much for the journalists' sake as his. They would be able to say they had done things right and avoid giving Weinstein an opening to say they'd been unfair.

To Baquet, that seemed like too much. Nobody in the group trusted Weinstein, but he was the most suspicious. His instincts told him that Weinstein was just going to run out the clock. Besides, the team figured that however long they gave Weinstein, he would take more time. This was a negotiation, and the journalists had to start on the short side.

But Baquet also wanted the investigation to be flawless. At the start of his newspaper career, he had covered the case of a small-time actor who was accused of rape. The way Baquet had written those stories still made him cringe all these years later. The man was guilty, Baquet was sure. But he had been too quick to convict him on the page, he thought, writing in a way that was too sensationalized and melodramatic, without enough fair summary of the arguments for the defense. "It was even probably disrespectful to the women," he said later. "I always felt like everyone in the courtroom lost a little respect for me, including the prosecutors." Baquet wanted to expose Weinstein, but correctly.

Everyone, including Jodi and Megan, took turns arguing every side, trying to weigh which risk was greater: compromising an investigation by moving too quickly in the final moments or being too generous to a proven manipulator. When the reporters stepped away to write more, the editors were still deliberating.

By the time darkness started to fall over Times Square, they had made a decision. Megan called Lanny Davis to put him on notice: she and Jodi wanted to speak to Weinstein and his team at one p.m. the following day to share the allegations.

Suddenly the journalists were as little as a day or two away from launch. All around them, colleagues were taking the small steps that turn a collection of words into a *Times* article. They needed the right picture of Weinstein for the top of the story and the front page, and Beth Flynn, the photo editor, sent a selection. Should he be smiling, not smiling? On a red carpet? With a woman—which woman? Was it a problem if his wife, Georgina Chapman, appeared in one of the shots? Come to think of it, should the article mention that he was married, for the second time, and that he had been married when most of the alleged transgressions occurred?

Only one journalist could log in to the story file at a time, so Jodi worked on the article, then Megan, then Rebecca Corbett, then Rory Tolan, a second editor taking an especially close look at language. They were trying to find the exact right phrasing and were rewriting based on notes from the *Times* lawyer David McCraw, who had offered recommendations to fireproof the story legally, so that Weinstein would be unlikely to win any libel suit against the paper.

Shortly after midnight, Megan and Jodi left the office and shared a car back to Brooklyn. For the first time, they allowed themselves to imagine how readers might react to the story. Megan suspected that the board of Weinstein's company would be forced to act against him, but would the broader world care? Jodi cited Purdy, who in classic skeptical-newspaper-editor fashion had pointed out earlier in the investigation that Harvey Weinstein wasn't that famous. Perhaps many people would find sleazy behavior by a Hollywood producer unsurprising.

Tuesday, October 3, 2017

As they prepared for the one p.m. call, Corbett received a peculiar message from Lanny Davis:

Dear Rebecca:

This is a very personal note.

I just learned about the Lauren email late last night and read it for the first time. Will do my best to do what should have been done a long time ago. I am not optimistic re. a statement. I am shooting for 1 pm today since that seems to be the absolute deadline. Correct me if I am wrong.

In any event, I thank you for your consideration and courtesy—way beyond what is customary or even necessary.

Lanny

To an outsider, the note might have seemed routine: sorry, I got some of the documents late; I'm just catching up and will do my best. Translated into the language of journalism and public relations, the note read this way:

Can you believe that Weinstein hired me to deal with your article but never even shared the Lauren O'Connor memo with me? This is embarrassing, and by the way, that memo is powerful. Bear with me, I'm trying to get Weinstein to give you some sort of a statement to print in the story, but this client is challenging.

David Boies would be unavailable to join the call, but he was still trying to intervene on Weinstein's behalf. At 12:19 p.m., Baquet received an email from the attorney, who was pushing for more time for Weinstein to respond in order "to make the article fair and balanced." Boies, who reiterated the claim that he was not Weinstein's lawyer in this matter, insinuated the *Times* should follow the lead of other media outlets.

"Three major publishers/broadcasters, including the *Times*, have researched this story over the last several months, and insofar as I can tell considered the same allegations and evidence," Boies wrote, in reference to NBC and the *New Yorker*. "One of the other two has said it has decided not to publish the story; the other has said that before they publish they will take the time to thoroughly review with Harvey the charges against him and give him adequate time to prepare a response. I would hope the *Times* would at least do the same."

"I'm not responding," Baquet told the reporters.

Just before one p.m., the reporters and Corbett settled in for the call. They had written out almost every word they planned to say.

Foremost on their minds were the women whose names they would be mentioning. In the hours beforehand, Jodi and Megan had warned Madden, Perkins, and the others, saying: we're about to go to Harvey for response, and we need to share every allegation in the article with him, including yours. I know this sounds scary, but it will protect you and us, because we can say this is a fair process that gives him a chance to respond to the charges. We don't think he or his representatives are likely to contact you. But carry around a notebook just in case, and if you get any calls, write down every word. Any threats or intimidation need to go straight into the article. The only way to combat those tactics is to expose them.

The women had agreed, their final act of trust.

When the call itself began, Weinstein was joined by not just Davis and Bloom but also a new lawyer, Charles Harder.

Harder had made a name attacking publications that criticized his wealthy or famous clients. Harder believed that libel laws, which governed who could say what about whom in print, were too loose. The prevailing legal standard had been established in 1964, when the Supreme Court decided in *New York Times Co. v. Sullivan* that a successful libel suit had to prove not only that journalists printed false information but that regarding public figures, they did so with "actual malice," defined as "reckless disregard for the truth." That was a high bar that generally protected journalists—too high a bar, Harder thought.

He had represented Roger Ailes in his efforts to beat back media coverage of Ailes's alleged sexual harassment. After he negotiated a $2.9 million settlement from the *Daily Mail* over a false report in 2016 about Melania Trump, President Trump hired him too. *GQ* magazine had recently called Harder "perhaps the greatest threat in the United States to journalists, the First Amendment, and the very notion of a free press."

On the phone, Harder was clipped and courteous, hearing out the reporters as they presented their material and repeating variations on "we'll get back to you."

His client had no such restraint. From the first moment of the call, Weinstein kept interrupting the reporters, intent on figuring out whom they had spoken to, who had betrayed him. Coming through the phone's speaker, his voice was even more of a force than it was in person, low, gravelly, and insistent, and he had a tactic of repeating the same question over and over. As Megan and Jodi went through the allegations, Weinstein tried to seize control with a stream of interjections:

"Who else is on the record?"

"Is there somebody on the record who said that?"

"Why don't you tell me who's on the record and let me respond to that?"

"And this woman's on the record?"

"And do you have somebody on the record who said this?"

He was so busy trying to grill the reporters that he did not seem to absorb the fact that the journalists had not just interviews but also settlement records and other documents, including the O'Connor memo.

Megan raised the crucial question of how many settlements Weinstein had paid out over the years. She had already heard the answer—eight to twelve—from Davis, but she needed a second source, and getting confirmation from Weinstein would be ideal. But when she cited the number Davis had given, Weinstein lashed out at his own adviser. "That's you talking; that's not me talking," he shot at Davis. "If Lanny spoke, he spoke for himself and not on behalf of his client," he said.

Megan tensed. The circle of people who knew about the settlements was tiny. Was that important figure slipping away?

When the journalists finished listing the allegations, Harder asked how much time they could take to respond. "Our expectation is that you can get back to us by the end of the day," Corbett said, as the editors had agreed.

"That's impossible," Harder shot back. "You're giving us three hours to respond to a laundry list of stuff going back to the early 1990s?" He asked for two weeks, which Corbett rejected, then he reduced his request to forty-eight hours. Corbett agreed to get back to him.

Weinstein's voice surged through the speaker again. "If the timing isn't good, then we will cooperate with someone else," he threatened, reading the journalists' fears that he would hang up from the call and go straight to another newspaper with a softened, distorted version of the story.

"I'm not a saint," Weinstein said, "but I'm not the sinner you think I am." He launched into a lecture about journalism.

"Get the facts right," he said. "We'll help you get the facts right. If I wasn't making movies, I would've been a journalist. I read every book on the *New York Times*, every book about journalism, and I read every newspaper and magazine. The journalists that impress me the most are the ones who go out of their way to be fair."

Weinstein went on. "When you were kids you grew up to tell the right story, to tell the truth," he continued. "You weren't about deadlines.

You wanted to tell the truth. If you mess up and you don't tell the truth, and you write just to write, how do you look yourself in the eye?"

Finally, after ninety minutes on the phone, it was over. Corbett and the reporters sat in the conference room.

Corbett was thinking about how to shore up some of the allegations to further strengthen the story and that the paper should agree to Harder's request for more time. An expert in Baquet's thinking, after years working with him, she was crafting an argument to share with him about a new deadline.

Megan was mentally reviewing Team Weinstein's reactions for clues about whether it had information that could refute or weaken the findings. Instead of addressing the grave matters at hand, Weinstein was asking questions that would not help his cause. He was fighting with Davis. He had been trying so hard to turn the tables that it was not clear how much of the information he had even processed.

Jodi was bracing for Weinstein's next move, certain he had a plan to use the information they had provided on the call to try to undermine the article. She felt sure what he would do: leak an item to the gossip pages saying, "The *New York Times* is trying to do a Harvey Weinstein story but barely got one woman on the record."

With one phone call, he could make the article seem like a failure before it was even published.

An hour later, Judd called Jodi.

The actress was as composed as ever. "I'm prepared to be a named source in your investigation," she said. She had thought deeply on the decision, gone for a run in the woods, consulted her lawyers, considered her obligations as a woman and a Christian, and decided this was just the right thing to do, she said.

Standing amid the neat lines of glass wall and gray carpet, Jodi lost it, like a marathoner collapsing at the finish line. She and Megan had spent months living in a state of suspense and responsibility. They would land the story or they would blow it; they would get actresses on the record or they would not. Weeping, Jodi searched for something to say to Judd that was equal to the moment but still professional. The best she could muster was: "This means the world to me as a journalist."

The rest of the team was standing down the hall in a cluster, and Jodi walked toward them, still on the phone with Judd, gesturing to say that she had news. Megan knew what was happening before Jodi could say it.

They celebrated by rewriting the story draft. The lede, or very opening of the article, was Judd's long-ago account from the Peninsula suite, and the first section of the article ended with a quote of Judd's that was also a call to action: "Women have been talking about Harvey amongst ourselves for a long time, and it's simply beyond time to have the conversation publicly." By that evening, they had a new version of the article, with Judd on the record. Meanwhile, Corbett prevailed: they would give Weinstein until noon the next day, Wednesday, October 4. That became the new target publication date for the article. Internally, the reporters set their clocks and expectations.

At nine o'clock that Tuesday night, the journalists were still at the office, eating takeout and sweating over the story draft. Their hum of anxiety was nothing compared to what was going on at The Weinstein Company, a few miles to the south, where Weinstein was on an emergency conference call with Boies and the board. Maerov had insisted on the meeting, outraged that Weinstein had hired lawyers and Davis's firm to deal with a story that the board knew nothing about.

Boies did most of the talking. After years of minimizing Weinstein's problems to the board, he was suddenly more forthright. The *Times* story was coming, he told them, and "it's going to be bad" for the company, participants in the call later recalled to Megan. He outlined the conclusions, including the eight to twelve settlements, adding that the number could very well be higher. He didn't think Weinstein in fact remembered how many payoffs he had made to women over the years, he said. Defending Weinstein or terminating him were both extreme and inappropriate, Boies argued. The goal was to find a middle ground and present a unified front. "Guys, if we don't stick together, this is going to be like a circular firing squad," he said.

By 11:38 p.m., Lisa Bloom was advising Weinstein to acknowledge that after all their efforts, they would not succeed in killing the *Times* story. "We can nip at it around the edges—and we should—but it is going to run," she wrote in an email to Weinstein, Harder, Davis, and Boies as she prepared to board a flight from Los Angeles to New York to be by her client's side. Bloom's pitch: Weinstein should acknowledge that he had engaged in the core issue of sexual harassment, express remorse, and promise to do better. In the email later obtained by Megan, Bloom proposed a statement to give to the *Times* that emphasized her own role and even her movie project:

"As a women's rights advocate, I have been blunt with Harvey and he has listened to me. I have told him that times have changed, it is 2017, and he needs to evolve to a higher standard. I have found Harvey to be refreshingly candid and receptive to my message. He has acknowledged mistakes he has made. And as we work together on a project bringing my book to the screen, he has always been respectful towards me."

Her message: she was the one who had helped Weinstein see the light.

After privately working to help Weinstein foil investigations into his behavior, she wanted to publicly cast herself as the person who forced him to change his ways.

For his own self-protection, Davis had decided to stay in Washington, DC. By then, he could tell that whatever Weinstein did, the producer would not be able to wiggle away from the article's findings. Even Boies was pushing contrition.

But Weinstein was not prepared to give in.

That day, Weinstein had called an IT staff member over to the computer of one of his executive assistants and ordered him to delete a document called "HW friends," according to people who were there. (That was essentially the same term Megan and Jodi's sources had used: "Friends of Harvey.") The document was a list of names and contact information for women categorized by city.

With the help of Bloom, Weinstein also tried to pressure employees into signing written declarations saying they had enjoyed a positive experience at the company.

The next morning, Megan checked in with the young woman who had left the company "for moral reasons." She explained by text message that Weinstein had called her three times that morning, suspecting she was a source.

"I'm scared," she wrote.

CHAPTER SEVEN

"THERE WILL BE A MOVEMENT"

Wednesday, October 4, 2017

THE REPORTERS CAME to work knowing they had to tell Team Weinstein that Judd was on the record but fearing the producer would weaponize the information somehow—use it to delay the response further or, worse, launch some sort of preemptive public smear campaign against Judd in the tabloids. ("Eccentric activist Ashley Judd has been threatening to go public with wild accusations . . .") But it had to be done. At 8:40 a.m., Jodi called Lanny Davis, who took the news stoically.

The phone call with Weinstein and his team the day before had dealt a potential blow to the crucial finding that Weinstein had struck settlements with as many as twelve women over the years. But now that other executives at The Weinstein Company knew the *Times* story was coming, Megan suspected they might be angry that Weinstein had jeopardized the company through his actions. Maybe that anger would drive them to talk.

Megan called David Glasser, The Weinstein Company president, in California. It wasn't yet dawn in Los Angeles, but Glasser picked up, sounding sleep-deprived and frazzled. Megan told him she was calling because she thought it only fair that other executives be given a chance to respond to the *Times* story.

Sure enough, Glasser acknowledged it had been a rough night. There had been an emergency board meeting by conference call. Boies had spelled out what the *Times* was preparing to publish, Glasser said, adding that he had been shocked by what he heard.

"Really?" Megan asked. What was most surprising? Did Boies mention the number of settlements Weinstein had paid to women? Yes, Glasser said: eight to twelve. Could she believe it? What's more, Boies had told the board the number might be even higher.

Megan told Glasser she was eager to include his perspective in the *Times* if and when he was ready to go on the record. Meantime, could she use him as a source for the settlement figure if she didn't name him? He agreed. When Megan told Corbett the news, Corbett jumped up from her seat and hugged her.

The journalists kept their eyes on the clock: the noon deadline was approaching. As it passed, Weinstein's team provided little more than a wild phone call, in which they sort of denied some of the allegations, rambled about episodes that weren't even in the article, and again protested that they didn't have enough time.

A few minutes later, Baquet watched as Megan stood outside his office fielding yet another phone call from Davis, who didn't have any answers. For so long, Baquet had refused to speak to Weinstein or any of his representatives. Now he had lost his patience and asked Megan to hand him her phone. "You've got five different lawyers reaching out to us," he said to Davis, his tone harder-edged than usual. "We're not talking to five different lawyers. Get your people in line and get back to us with your response."

At 1:43 p.m., Team Weinstein's answer landed, in the form of an emailed letter from Charles Harder marked "CONFIDENTIAL / OFF THE RECORD / NOT FOR PUBLICATION." The journalists didn't consider that binding, because keeping material off the record required agreement on their part—it had to be a two-way deal, not a command. But it was a fitting start to the letter, an eighteen-page exercise in intimidation, all of which boiled down to one message: if the journalists proceeded, Weinstein and Harder would sue the *Times*.

The core team reassembled in Baquet's office. David McCraw handed out printed copies so everyone could review what they were facing. "Demand to Cease & Desist and Preserve Documents and Materials," the subject line said. For all those months—and in the previous few days in particular—they had been waiting to see what stance Weinstein would ultimately take: denial or apology. Now they saw the answer on the page:

> All accusations by NYT and its alleged "sources" that my client engaged in sexual harassment, including toward employees and actors, are untrue. My client did not engage in the wrongful conduct that you are accusing him of.
>
> My client would likely incur more than $100 million in damage from your false story. Should you publish it, he would have no alternative but to hold NYT legally responsible for those damages.

Weinstein and Harder had another, more tactical demand:

> Because these accusations will have the effect, as you know,
> of causing considerable damage, if not total destruction, to
> the highly successful career and business that my client has
> built over the past forty years, and because you have been
> working on this story about him for several months now, and
> the alleged events go back more than 25 years in time, at
> the very least it would be appropriate for NYT to afford my
> client and his counsel with a reasonable amount of time—we
> request two weeks—to research these issues and make an
> appropriate presentation of the facts and evidence which
> refute the many false accusations that NYT is prepared to
> publish about my client. A court of law affords a defendant at
> least a year to conduct discovery and present their case at
> trial. We are asking you for two weeks.

Weinstein was going to fight. According to the letter, he was the real victim, pursued by the *Times*. The letter, seething with contempt for journalism, conjured a dark alternative reality in which newspapers that aired negative information about the powerful were violating—not upholding—the public trust.

The letter took direct aim at Laura Madden, calling her a liar. "The accusation is false," Harder wrote:

> We expect to be able to provide you with documents and
> witnesses that will refute this allegation, but it will take us

> time to locate documents and witnesses from 25 years
> ago. You are now on notice of the truth. Should you publish
> this false accusation before my client has had a reasonable
> opportunity to locate and present to you further evidence
> (witnesses and documents) of the falsity of this allegation,
> will easily demonstrate reckless disregard for the truth.

That phrase was how a plaintiff—a person suing—could win a libel suit: by proving that journalists had heard their information was false and had maliciously published anyway.

Jodi thought of Madden, somewhere in Wales. If Weinstein had any kind of genuine refutation of her story, some way to conclusively prove he hadn't been there or done what she alleged, she needed to know about it immediately. Or was he just gambling, thinking that this was just one woman with no power and little proof, and that his best bet was just to deny?

The former employees helping the reporters were "disgruntled, have ulterior motives, and seek to supply you with false and defamatory statements," the letter said. "You are on notice that your sources are not reliable; they do not have personal information; and they are seeking to use NYT as a vehicle" to hurt Weinstein and his company. "The publication of any such false accusations about my client by NYT will be with actual malice and constitute defamation." There was the possibility that Team Weinstein would try to publicly cast the gutsy ex-employees as bitter outcasts, losers.

In the final section, Weinstein and Harder took direct aim at Jodi and Megan:

Please be advised that you are under a legal duty to
maintain, preserve, protect, and not destroy any and
all documents, communications, materials and data,
in digital, electronic and hard copy form, that may be
relevant to the dispute including without limitation all
documents, materials and data that refer or relate to
Harvey Weinstein, The Weinstein Company and/or
any of its executives, employees and/or contractors
(collectively, "TWC").

That meant everything: every text, instant message, voice mail,
calendar entry. Harvey Weinstein was saying he was going to force the
Times to turn over the entire contents of the investigation, everything
the reporters were sworn to protect.

The journalists sat in Baquet's office and came to a unified decision:
there was no reason to change a single element of the story. Harder's
letter was essentially legalistic bullying. The journalists would stay
open to whatever evidence Weinstein wanted to present, but to capitu-
late based on this letter was unthinkable.

McCraw reassured the group that the law would protect them. The
world that Harder had conjured up sounded scary, but it didn't actually
exist. "When the facts protect us, and the law protects us, it's hard to
argue with our legal position," McCraw said later.

At 3:33 p.m., McCraw forwarded the reporters a copy of the reply
he had just sent to Harder, just three paragraphs long. To the eighteen
pages of complaints about journalistic technique, McCraw had a simple
answer: "Any notion that we have dealt unfairly with Mr. Weinstein is

simply false, and you can be sure that any article we do will meet our customary standards for accuracy and fairness."

In the final paragraph, he delivered his real counterpunch:

> I note your document preservation demands. In light of that, please provide me with assurances that you have taken immediate steps to secure all data and records that may be relevant to this matter, whether in the possession, custody, and control of Mr. Weinstein or one of his business entities. In particular, I ask that you immediately secure all phone, email and text records of Mr. Davis, Mr. Weinstein's press representative, as well as the personal and business phone, email and text accounts of Mr. Weinstein; all records pertaining to any complaints of improper workplace behavior, whether in the possession, custody and control of Mr. Weinstein or one of his business entities; and all records relating to settlements with employees, whether in the possession, custody and control of Mr. Weinstein or one of his business entities.

Translated from legalese, this meant: Harvey Weinstein, if you want to drag this story into open court, go right ahead. If you try to come after our information, we will demand even more of yours, including every single document related to your treatment of women.

The paper's one concession was to give Weinstein more time. Two weeks was out of the question. But the journalists felt they had to say yes to Harder's earlier request of forty-eight hours, even though it was painful to leave the material hanging with Weinstein for so long. Anything less could give credence to his argument about unfairness. The new and final deadline would be one p.m. the following day, Thursday, October 5.

Jodi and Megan were exhausted, but McCraw's response gave them a boost. He had invoked generations of journalistic tradition, a court system that still protected the free press, and a country where, despite everything, the First Amendment was still untouchable. They also realized that Baquet was savoring each moment of the face-off with Weinstein. The rest of the world could not see Harder's offensive. But standing together against it was thrilling.

That afternoon, Jodi felt she had to try one last time to convince Paltrow to go on the record. Hearing from his former top star would be so shocking to readers across the world; even many of the reporters' savviest sources did not expect that Paltrow had a story of being victimized or threatened by Weinstein. Three paragraphs about her could rewrite the history of the Miramax years and give cover to so many of the other women who wanted to come forward. Jodi summoned every last bit of persuasion she had, pushing so hard that she worried the pressure would backfire and that the star was going to tell her to get lost.

The two had been in near-constant dialogue for a week, in phone calls and texts, and Paltrow seemed to be truly deliberating. She had helped with the project from their first contact. But everyone close to her was telling her to stay quiet. Of course, going on the record sounded crazy to them: they were not on the inside of the investigation. Jodi could tell that some part of Paltrow wanted to ignore them, so in phone calls and texts, she continued to gently push.

But Paltrow couldn't bear the thought of weeks of tabloid headlines about her, Weinstein, and sex. She was still afraid the news would devolve into a lurid celebrity scandal.

> Since I feel underequipped to make this decision under a barrel, I'm going to hold.

> I feel sorry to have let you down. I really do. I'm so torn.

Paltrow's dissatisfaction with her own decision meant that if she did not join this article, Jodi wanted her to be ready for the next one; she could watch from the wings and then enter. Jodi let up with the texts for a few hours, and then started again.

From the beginning, Jodi and Megan had stuck to Baquet's rule: all communication with Weinstein had to be on the record. But around three p.m., Megan was informed by Davis that Weinstein was already on his way to share some sensitive, crucial information off the record.

The reporters were confused. He was on his way where? To the office? Should they refuse to let him in? They had to make a choice fast: Weinstein would be on their doorstep in minutes, no doubt looking to smear his accusers without leaving fingerprints.

Megan decided to take the meeting. She wanted to know what he had, and the dirty trick of the impromptu meeting gave her another chance to square off against him in person.

Weinstein stepped into the lobby of the *Times*, with an unshaven face, bags under his eyes, and high-profile legal help by his side: not just Bloom but also Abramowitz, the former prosecutor turned criminal attorney who had represented Weinstein in the Gutierrez case. Bringing up the rear was Linda Fairstein, the former sex crimes prosecutor who had told Megan there was nothing to Gutierrez's allegations.

Megan led the group to one of the newsroom's small glass-walled meeting rooms along a heavily trafficked corridor, which put Weinstein on display for all of their colleagues to see. Office passersby lingered at the sight of the producer and his representatives stuffed in the equivalent of a fishbowl. Megan told Weinstein and company that they had fifteen minutes to talk, not a minute more.

The information the group sought to supply was nasty, dubious, and thin. Abramowitz and Fairstein painted Gutierrez as an opportunist with a sleazy past. From a folder, Bloom pulled out pictures of McGowan and Judd smiling alongside Weinstein, as if polite red-carpet photos were proof that nothing bad had happened. Weinstein accused both women of being mentally unstable. At one point, Judd had sought in-patient psychological treatment for issues stemming from her childhood, and now the producer used descriptions from her own memoir to paint her as a nut. They couldn't disprove the accusations the women made. Their best attempt to shut down the article was to smear the women.

Megan betrayed as little reaction as possible. This off-the-record meeting had clearly been an ambush, but it did nothing to undermine the investigation. With the help of a colleague in Italy, Jodi and Megan had done background checks of Gutierrez. They had also examined

Judd's history, asking Grace Ashford, the researcher, to plow through her memoir, just to make sure there were no surprises that could be used against her or the paper. The only thing the meeting had done was reveal more of the tactics Weinstein and his allies were prepared to use.

The day got stranger. That afternoon, Jodi and Megan sat down to read about themselves in *Variety* and the *Hollywood Reporter*:

IS THE *NEW YORK TIMES* ABOUT TO EXPOSE DAMAGING INFORMATION ON HARVEY WEINSTEIN?

The Weinstein Co. film and television mogul has enlisted an army of attorneys and crisis managers in recent weeks and has unleashed them on the *Times* over a planned story on his personal behavior, multiple sources familiar with the behind-the-scenes battle tell the *Hollywood Reporter*.

The story had few details but did mention the *New Yorker*'s efforts as well. *Variety*'s article was similar, with Weinstein denying that he even knew about an upcoming *Times* story. "I've not been aware of this," Weinstein told *Variety*. "I don't know what you're talking about, honestly."

"The story sounds so good I want to buy the movie rights," he added. If the reporters had any remaining doubts about Weinstein's integrity, here was a final sign: he had just told another publication a flat-out lie.

The *Variety* and *Hollywood Reporter* stories meant that Jodi and Megan were on public display. The guessing games about who had spoken to them would begin. Sources would get nervous. The project was exposed for everyone to see, including the competition. Right when the reporters needed the tightest possible control, they were losing it.

"This is bad, gang," Baquet wrote in an email.

The reporters' phones and inboxes began to fill with messages from people who had seen the stories in the Hollywood trade publications. Jodi and Megan barely responded. They were still too deep in the text of the article, reworking the lede again, targeting problem areas, and carrying out McCraw's instructions for further fine-tuning.

Sometime after midnight, the reporters realized they were too wiped out to be effective anymore. They had gone with little sleep for many nights in a row. The conversations with Corbett and Tolan were sputtering in circles. Jodi and Megan gave up and shared a taxi home. About an hour later, Tolan left too. Corbett refused to pull away from the keyboard. They had fiddled so much with various parts of the article that Corbett wanted to stop to reread the whole story and measure what could still be gained and strengthened on the page.

Even under more routine circumstances, Corbett's reporters worried that she did not take care of herself. She never seemed to stop working—because many of her projects were secret, it was hard to gauge how much she was really fielding—and at times appeared to survive on black tea and dark-chocolate-covered almonds. Her days were frenzied, with consultations every few minutes.

But in the hush of a newsroom finally drained of activity, she was able to edit stories with real concentration. (Being "in the zone," her husband called it, acknowledging that his wife was temporarily inaccessible.) Corbett often stayed at work so long that the ceiling lights sometimes automatically clicked off, leaving her working in darkness until she got up and waved her arms.

That night, she sat and worked away, slowly making the words in the story tighter, clearer, and stronger. Sometime before dawn, she fell asleep at her desk for forty-five minutes. When she woke, she worked some more. At seven a.m., she finally stopped and left the building. She couldn't go home: Corbett lived in Baltimore, spending every Tuesday through Friday in a hotel room down the street from the *Times*. She showered and changed her clothing. Soon afterward, she was back at her desk.

Thursday, October 5, 2017

Just as Corbett was returning to her hotel, Jodi received an email from Laura Madden, who was now five days away from her surgery. The previous evening, she had stood in her kitchen in Wales and told her older two daughters, Gracie and Nell, that she had to share something. The teenagers assumed it was about the operation. Instead Madden told them what Weinstein had done to her all those years before and that the incident was about to be recounted in a newspaper article.

They looked at her in shock, trying to picture her as a twenty-year-old victim. "My mom is just my mom," Gracie said. "She's such a gentle person. The idea that people could be reading what happened to her . . ." They confessed to Madden that similar things had recently happened to some of their girlfriends: drunken boys preying on them, the young women unsure what to do. It was Madden's turn to be shocked. She knew these kids but had never dreamed of what they were facing.

In the email, Madden wrote to Jodi:

> I feel obliged to talk about the events that happened
> to me at Miramax as I realise that I'm in the fortunate
> position of not being employed in the film business and
> so my livelihood won't be affected. I'm also not one of
> those that have been silenced even though individuals
> under Harvey Weinstein have tried to persuade me to be
> silent. I do not have a gagging order against me either.
> I feel I am speaking out on behalf of women who can't
> because their livelihoods or marriages may be affected.
> I am the mother of 3 daughters and I do not want
> them to have to accept this kind of bullying behaviour
> in any setting as "normal." I have been through life
> changing health issues and know that time is precious
> and confronting bullies is important. My family are all
> supportive of my decision.
>
> I am happy to go on record.

Just as remarkably, Jodi and Megan were starting to hear from women they had never contacted who had their own Weinstein stories they wanted to share. For months the reporters had been pursuing women, aching for them to speak. Now they were coming to Jodi and Megan, finding them through the *Variety* and *Hollywood Reporter* articles, like a river suddenly flowing in the opposite direction. The journalists did not have enough time to do the reporting, corroboration, and response to include their accounts in the first article. They would have to wait for the next story. But the journalists took the messages as a silent answer to Harder's letter.

At ten thirty a.m., Jodi gave Paltrow one final try. She was sitting in a makeup chair in Atlanta, shooting an Avengers movie. That day she was supposed to pose for a big Avengers class photo, with all the characters from the preceding decade. Instead she was feeling sick and barely able to get through her scenes. She even pulled aside Michelle Pfeiffer, her costar, quickly briefing her on the situation for one final round of counsel.

At 11:22 a.m., she sent Jodi a text.

> I'm on set in Atlanta. I feel intense pressure because of the time frame. I can't believe his response to the Hollywood Reporter, I can't believe he is taking this tack. I would have hoped he could have seen his way to contrition. I feel like he's setting himself up for an even steeper fall.

> I think it will be best to hold and then do something with you as a follow up.

This made the email that arrived from Davis at 12:04 p.m. especially puzzling. Weinstein's team had fifty-six minutes left on the clock until the *Times*'s deadline. But instead of focusing on the many allegations that would be in the article, Weinstein, through Davis, was pelting the reporters with questions about Paltrow, who he seemed convinced was in the story.

Jodi and Megan were dumbfounded. There was no trace of Paltrow in the story—if there had been, they would have asked him for comment as they had with Judd's accusations. Why was he focusing on an irrelevant matter? Had he never intended to give any response to the allegations at all? One o'clock came and went. Team Weinstein insisted the statements were almost finished, but by 1:33 p.m., nothing had arrived.

Baquet watched as Megan fielded yet another phone call from Davis, who once again had nothing to offer. Baquet instructed Megan to deliver a message. "Tell Lanny the deadline has passed!"

Suddenly, Weinstein himself was on the phone, asking about Paltrow, angrily asserting that he would hang up and do an interview with the *Washington Post*. "I will do that interview in the next five minutes unless you come clean. If you don't want to come clean, you'd better write this fast."

Megan and Jodi were back in one of the glass-box conference rooms.

Outside, Corbett and Purdy hovered over Tolan's shoulder, reviewing the article.

"You want some sort of list of who we've spoken to for this story?" Jodi asked. "And if we don't disclose it to you, you're threatening us?"

"I'm not threatening you," he said. "If you're using Gwyneth Paltrow, tell me." However scared Paltrow was of going on the record, he seemed much more fearful.

"We're not using Gwyneth Paltrow," Megan said. He did not seem to understand: if Paltrow were in the story, they would have told him so and given him time to respond.

He asked twice more, then a third time. "If you're going to lie to me, don't, okay? Just don't. You're going to slaughter me anyhow, that's the idea of it. I get it. And you know what? I respect your journalism, and I respect what you're doing. You're dealing with an important subject matter, and people like me need to learn and grow. I get that. You'll read that in my statement. I've known when I hear something that's hidden from me, you know what I mean? I am a man who has great resources. Tell me the truth." He did seem certain that Jodi and Megan had been speaking with Paltrow. Even months later, they never figured out how he knew.

Megan tried again: "Harvey, we have not robbed you of the opportunity to speak to anything that's in our story," she said.

"Are you talking to Gwyneth Paltrow?" Weinstein repeated.

A figure appeared next to Megan. Dean Baquet was leaning over her shoulder. So many times over the prior few months, Weinstein had wanted to reach him directly, influence him, Important Man to Important Man. Now Weinstein was finally getting the audience he wanted.

"Hey, Harvey? This is Dean Baquet," he started. "Here's the deal. You need to give us your statement now. I'm about to push the button."

Weinstein interrupted. "Hey, Dean, let me tell you something about intimidation." The producer repeated the threat to give the *Washington Post* an interview, to undercut the *Times* story. Baquet had been a journalist for nearly four decades, run two of the country's top newspapers, and gone up against the CIA and foreign dictators. Was he about to explode?

Instead his voice eased, the slight New Orleans lilt returning. "Harvey, call them," he said. "That's fine. You can call the *Post*." He sounded like he was reassuring a child. "Harvey, I'm not trying to intimidate you; I'm trying to be fair with you."

"You are intimidating me, Dean," Weinstein said.

Now Corbett and Purdy were in the room too. "No, Harvey, here's the deal," Baquet said. "We're trying to get your statement to be fair. Please give it to us now because we're about to publish."

"I want to give it to you," Weinstein said.

"Thank you," Baquet said, hoping for finality.

"But while you're on the phone, this is my career, my life," Weinstein said. He started asking about Paltrow again.

"She's not in the story," Baquet, Megan, and Jodi said nearly in unison. "Harvey, I'm about to end this part of the conversation," Baquet said.

"So here's what we need to do now, Harvey. We want to give you every word that you want to say. So say it. I also have a newspaper to put out. So give them your statement. I'm going to walk out. Talk to the reporters. Take care. Good luck." And with that, he left.

A minute later, at 1:41 p.m., multiple statements from Weinstein's team began arriving—the final elements the journalists needed to be able to publish.

On the phone, Weinstein was still making speeches ("Even if it costs me at the end of the day, investigations like this are important"), and Bloom was complaining that the paper had "a reckless disregard for the truth" and was going to publish "a hit piece" filled with "false accusations," which would soon be discredited. Corbett and Purdy had slipped out of the room without the reporters noticing.

Megan, who was scanning the statements from the Weinstein side, suddenly saw something important in the text in front of her and interjected. "Lisa, you said that Harvey needs time off to focus on this issue?"

Yes, Weinstein said. He was going to take time off.

"From . . . the company?" Megan asked, wanting to make sure this was what she thought it was. Yes, Weinstein said, he wanted to spend some time learning.

"Learning and listening to me," Bloom chimed in.

Weinstein was still talking, advising Jodi and Megan that they needed more of a sense of humor, and that he prayed every single day for the *New York Times*.

But Megan and Jodi were looking at one another in wonder. Weinstein was taking a leave of absence from his company. In the language of journalism, public relations, and business, that meant one thing: he was admitting wrongdoing. No one took a leave of absence from his own company when he was planning on fighting with full force. Suddenly, the reporters knew he probably wasn't going to sue the paper or even challenge the article much.

Megan pushed him for more specifics on his plans, but he promised to call back later. "We have the Chinese newspaper to do the press conference with," Weinstein joked, wisecracking about his threat to take the story to a competing publication.

Megan laughed out loud.

"She laughed!" Weinstein exclaimed. "They laughed for the first time," he said to Bloom. Maybe this was the rough charm others had tried to explain. Or perhaps Weinstein was looking for one moment of dominance and control amid his own ruination.

It didn't matter. Megan and Jodi hung up from the call and fell together, laughing and crying with relief, camaraderie, and sisterhood.

———

The reporters came out of the glass conference room ready to go. But Corbett and the other editors were already far ahead of them. They had been editing as the call was taking place, examining the statements of the Weinstein team, lifting out the crucial material to use, and transplanting those lines into the article.

Together, the written statements of Weinstein and his lawyers were baffling. Lisa Bloom's statement denied "many of the accusations as patently false," but she didn't say which. Weinstein's was vaguely sorry ("I realized some time ago that I needed to be a better person ... My journey now will be to learn about myself and conquer my demons . . . I so respect all women and regret what happened.") In rambling paragraphs, he talked of working against the National Rifle Association and referenced nonexistent Jay-Z lyrics.

"I'm making a movie about our president, perhaps we can make it a joint retirement party." It was the most incoherent, least professional statement any of the journalists could remember.

"He wasn't intimidating, really, he was just a screamer," Matt Purdy said. "He had a lot of lawyers. He had a lot of words. He had a big voice. But we had all the facts."

Now the two reporters and three editors lined up behind Tolan, who sat at the keyboard, all of their eyes reviewing the article on his computer screen. The old way of publishing newspaper stories was to send them to presses with giant rolls of paper and vats of ink, and then rumbling trucks, then newsstands and lawns. The new way was to push a single button.

Baquet, jumping out of his skin, thought the story was ready to go. Purdy suggested that the six journalists read through it together one last time.

They started at the top, with the headline:

HARVEY WEINSTEIN PAID OFF SEXUAL HARASSMENT ACCUSERS FOR DECADES

The article started by stacking three separate stories from the Peninsula Hotel. The reporters had the reference to at least eight settlements, and the string of allegations they had worked to document, starting with the young assistant in New York in 1990, then Madden in Ireland, the terrible pattern continuing until 2015. "Dozens of Mr. Weinstein's former and current employees, from assistants to top executives, said they knew of inappropriate conduct while they worked for him. Only a handful said they ever confronted him," they had written. The article described the way women who had come forward had been shut down or silenced.

The team read every line in silent unison. When they finished, no one had any fixes or suggestions. At 2:05 p.m., only twenty-four minutes after Weinstein sent his statements, Tolan pushed the button.

After months of collecting information, locating and talking to sources, poring over records and emails, piecing together this puzzle, the article was out in the world. Jodi and Megan were elated and tense. Happy that the piece was finally published, but worried for their sources, especially those on the record, about how it would impact their lives. The women had trusted Jodi and Megan with their most personal stories. Would they face retaliation?

Weinstein had not grasped that the article would be published right away. At that moment, he was in his office with Bloom and other defenders, planning their next move, when an assistant popped his head in. "The story's up," he told them. Employees throughout the office became fixed to their computer screens, taking in the news about their boss.

Back at the *Times*, Jodi's phone rang. "I have Harvey Weinstein for you," an assistant said in a routine singsong.

"There was no sexual harassment in the room with Ashley Judd," Weinstein bellowed as soon as he got on the line. "There was no police report. This is a dead issue."

Jodi and Megan asked him if he planned to retaliate against the women whose names appeared in the story. They wanted that answer on the record.

"The retaliation is going to be about your reporting," he said. His joking tone from an hour before had turned more menacing, and then it switched again. "I'm sorry to the women too," he said. "I'm no saint, we all know." On the phone, as in the statements, he was hopping between denial and remorse and back again. How could the *Times* call his actions harassment, he wanted to know, if the girls had come up to his hotel room?

The final notes he played were of self-pity. "I'm already dead. I'm already dead," he said. "I'm going to be a rolling stone."

The thirty-three-hundred-word article triggered an immediate crisis for The Weinstein Company. Within hours, the company's board convened an emergency meeting by conference call to determine how to respond, according to notes made from an audio recording of the meeting later obtained by Megan.

An enraged Bob Weinstein and several other board members

insisted his brother follow through with a leave of absence and more mental-health treatment while the company investigated his conduct. But Weinstein pushed back, making it sound like the statement he provided to the *Times* was more show than substance. The board was engaging in a "rush to judgment." In retaliation, he would use his connections to launch a negative story about Maerov in the *Wall Street Journal*. Weinstein refused to submit to an investigation that would "put me in jail." He would sell the company before being pushed out. "I will not be railroaded," he told the board.

But after so many years of clouded vision and compromise, Bob Weinstein finally had a clear view of his brother and what the story meant for him. "You are finished, Harvey," he told him.

In the following days, most of the directors would resign without making public comment. But in this private meeting, their views were on display. Richard Koenigsberg, a onetime accountant to the Weinstein brothers, proposed that the company's board walk a "fine line: we don't approve of the behavior, but we can't be held responsible for what Harvey Weinstein did twenty years ago." Tim Sarnoff, of the production and distribution company Technicolor, thought it would be impossible to disconnect Weinstein from his company, and, as a result, the directors "need to protect Harvey." Paul Tudor Jones, an investor, sounded at times downright optimistic, convinced "it will be forgotten."

Even at that late hour, they sounded more concerned with the welfare of the company than the welfare of the women, which had been the problem all along. By focusing so narrowly on liability—the potential for a lawsuit—they had allowed the problem to grow and ultimately destroy what they had sought to protect.

During that board meeting, Weinstein was already touting a comeback narrative, with the help of Lisa Bloom. He said they would win the support of women's organizations, forty, fifty, sixty of them.

"There will be a movement," Weinstein asserted.

That evening at 9:07 p.m., Bloom wrote a defiant email to the board, her conciliatory tone from her statement to the *Times* gone.

This is the worst day.

This is the day the *New York Times* came out with a largely false and defamatory piece, in a major violation of journalistic ethics, giving only two days to respond to dozens of allegations, and then refusing to include information about eyewitnesses and documents negating many of the claims.

Tomorrow there will be more and different reporting, highlighting inaccuracies, including photos of several of the accusers in very friendly poses with Harvey after his alleged misconduct.

Bloom's note falsely suggested that Weinstein's team had disproved the claims. They had played their best cards when they came into the newsroom the day before, and all they had was a flimsy collection of smears and the threat of a lawsuit. Bloom was right though about more reporting. It just wasn't the kind she envisioned.

On the next day, Friday, October 6, Jodi and Megan began hearing from so many women with Weinstein stories that Corbett recruited other colleagues to help call them all back. The women described harassment, rape, assault, going back to the 1970s. Jodi and Megan faced a question they never thought they would contemplate: How many Weinstein victims could they actually write about?

After the *Times* article was published, Ronan Farrow was finishing his own powerful, detailed account of Weinstein offenses, and other reports surfaced.

Angelina Jolie's representatives arranged a time for her and Jodi to speak. And Paltrow was also ready to join the next *Times* article, about Weinstein's harassment and how orchestrated it was—"meetings," business discussions, assistants, the promise of stardom as a means of predation.

"This way of treating women ends now," she said in the new article that Jodi and a colleague were just beginning to write.

Lisa Bloom suffered through an uncomfortable appearance on *Good Morning America*, which appeared even more awkward when Megan later revealed in the paper that Bloom had promised The Weinstein Company board publication of photos of Weinstein's accusers posing with him. By then, Bloom had resigned from Weinstein's team, as had Lanny Davis. Now Megan was pressing forward, determined to learn more about what Weinstein's companies knew about the allegations against him and when.

The only person who did not hear much of the escalating roar of reaction was Ashley Judd. Just before publication, she had left for the Great Smoky Mountains National Park to go camping alone. She had almost no cell reception, had made a vow not to check Twitter, and asked her representatives to deal with whatever inquiries came in. About once a day, when she got a few bars of cell service, she sent Jodi pictures of serene, lush mountain landscapes. Hiking amid the dogwoods and magnolias, she had only hints of how her statements about Weinstein had been received and whether the story had meant something to others as well.

CHAPTER EIGHT

AFTERWARD

THE WEINSTEIN STORY stripped away the binds of secrecy, freeing women all over the world to speak up about similar experiences. The name Harvey Weinstein came to represent an argument for addressing misconduct, lest it go unchecked for decades. An example of how less-severe misbehaviors could lead to more serious ones. An emerging consensus that speaking up about sexual harassment and abuse was admirable, not shameful or disloyal. A cautionary tale about how that kind of behavior could become a grave risk for employers. Most of all, it marked an emerging agreement that Weinstein-like conduct was unquestionably wrong and should not be tolerated.

The aftermath was like nothing Jodi and Megan had ever imagined. In the weeks after the first article on Weinstein, an overwhelming surge of tips flowed into the *Times* and other news organizations—a messy, unexamined, alarming record of what women in the US and beyond said they had endured. The investigations became a project across journalism. The *Times* sexual harassment team expanded, digging into the stories of restaurant waitstaff, ballet dancers, domestic and factory workers, Google employees, models, prison guards, and many others.

That autumn, women from every arena of life posted #MeToo stories on social media, coming forward in new solidarity and of their own choosing—without the months of trust-building or persuasion required in the Weinstein investigation. Late one night when Megan took a break from working to absorb the declarations on her own social media accounts, the sight of such posts from women she knew made her weep.

The key to change was a new sense of accountability: as women gained confidence that telling their stories would lead to action, more of them opened up. The volume and pain of those stories showed the scale of the problem and the way it had overturned lives and undermined workplace progress. Businesses and other institutions investigated and fired their own leaders. Those consequences—the promise that telling the truth could lead to action—persuaded yet more women to speak up.

There were revolts in state legislatures over long-buried allegations. Swarms of protestors in the streets of Stockholm. The resignation of the British minister of defense. The instant professional evaporation of men whose power had seemed fixed: the television hosts Charlie Rose and Matt Lauer and the celebrity chef Mario Batali. Growing consensus that all sorts of previously tolerated practices were wrong: sexual overtures from the boss, corporate policies that kept harassment and abuse secret, and even smaller-scale behaviors like bra snapping in school hallways and laughing at movie scenes in which girls were taken advantage of by conquering male heroes. So much was suddenly open to question. The reckoning, and the feeling of rapidly shifting social standards, seemed like a sign that progress was still possible, even at a time of political division and nonstop conflict.

In its first few months, the post-Weinstein reckoning mostly transcended partisan politics: Republicans fell and Democrats too. The offenses were universal and forced many people into self-examination. It felt like a fresh break from the depressing old formula that had dominated the public conversations around the allegations against men on the left and right, which were characterized by opinion split along party lines, and results something more like holy wars than true moral accountings.

So much was surfacing so suddenly, and so many people were asking: What had really happened in the past? What had been concealed? Who was responsible?

Seven months after their first piece on Weinstein's alleged misdeeds had been published, Jodi and Megan sat in a Manhattan courtroom. They were waiting for Weinstein, who had spent that morning at a precinct house a few blocks away being booked, fingerprinted, and recorded in a series of mug shots.

The producer had already lost his job and reputation. But that day he would begin to face the ultimate accountability. Outside the courthouse, long lines of cameras were waiting, strangely reminiscent of the red carpets he had walked for so long.

With the bars of a holding cell momentarily visible behind him, Weinstein entered the courtroom in a posture of humiliation. His arms were immobilized behind his back with three sets of handcuffs to accommodate his large size, and he was led by two detectives, one of them female. The judge called the proceeding to order, and the female prosecutor called out the counts, her voice ringing out: "Your honor, the defendant is before the court, charged with two violent B felonies for two separate forcible assaults." In a brief few minutes, Weinstein was charged with raping one woman and forcing another into a sexual act. He surrendered his freedom, in the form of his passport, before posting a million dollars' bail, which would keep him out of jail as he awaited his trial.

There was no way of predicting the outcome of the trial. Weinstein could not be tried for sexual harassment. That was a civil offense, and though many women had filed lawsuits against him, it was unclear how those would be resolved. Some of the most serious criminal allegations against the producer were not represented that day and would never land in court because they were beyond New York's statute of limitations—they were alleged to have taken place too long ago to be prosecuted now. Other alleged victims had thus far chosen not to cooperate with the authorities, intent on protecting themselves or pessimistic that Weinstein would be convicted. Jodi and Megan had not checked out the two women behind the day's charges; they were among the dozens who came forward after the *Times* story broke, and one woman's name had not even been made public. (Later, prosecutors dropped a set of charges based on one of those accusers, then added another set related to a third alleged victim.) Sex crimes were notoriously difficult to try in court, and Weinstein's defense attorney was promising he would win.

But after nearly fifty years of alleged misdeeds, prosecutors finally had Weinstein in their sights. "He's now experiencing all the things he's put everybody else through," Cynthia Burr, one of his accusers, told the

Times. "Humiliation, worthlessness, fear, weakness, aloneness, loss, suffering and embarrassment. And it's only the beginning for him."

In the final moments of his day in court, Weinstein was given a bulky electronic ankle bracelet to monitor his whereabouts. He protested, fighting the inevitable, then gave up: What choice did he have? When he exited the courtroom, Weinstein looked dazed, as if he was still absorbing what had happened.

As spring turned to summer of 2018, Jodi and Megan began to focus on a new question: How much was truly changing, and was it too much or not nearly enough?

The old rules on sex and power had been partly swept away, but it was not clear what the new ones would or should be. There was little agreement, and heated debate, over what behaviors were under scrutiny, how to know what to believe, and what accountability should look like. Years before, Tarana Burke had started the #MeToo movement to promote empathy and healing for victims of sexual violence, but now that label was being used as a catchall for a huge range of complaints, from verbal abuse to uncomfortable dates, many of which lacked the clarity of workplace or criminal violations. Earlier that year, babe.net, an online magazine, published an article accusing the comedian Aziz Ansari of behaving badly in a private romantic situation. But it was hard to tell whether his behavior was just overeager and clueless or worse.

That story was based entirely on one incident, recounted by an anonymous accuser, highlighting another dilemma: though many publications continued to publish exposés based on in-depth investigation and on-the-record evidence, others were running stories that relied on a single source or unnamed accusers, much lower standards. Once published, some of those stories flushed out additional allegations and more evidence of wrongdoing. But other stories appeared thin and one-sided, raising questions of fairness to those facing accusations. So did allegations leveled on social media without any backup or response from the accused.

"Believe women" grew into one of the catchphrases of the day. Jodi and Megan were sympathetic to the spirit behind that imperative: they had spent their careers getting women's stories into print. But the obligation of journalists was to scrutinize, verify, check, and question information. (A former editor of Megan's displayed a sign on his desk that read: IF YOUR MOTHER TELLS YOU SHE LOVES YOU, CHECK IT OUT.) The Weinstein story had impact in part because it had achieved something that, in 2018, seemed rare and precious: broad consensus on the facts.

Accountability was easy to insist on, but in some cases, much trickier to assign. Many companies, mindful of the lessons of The Weinstein Company's failures to act, started boasting of zero tolerance policies, but for what: An unwelcome hand placed on a back? A stray drunken comment at a holiday party? More and more critics were complaining that men were becoming the victims.

Even Weinstein's then attorney, Benjamin Brafman, seized on the criticism. In June 2018, a month after Weinstein was charged, Brafman gave a radio interview in which he articulated the rising sense of grievance. He argued that the charges against Weinstein were just another way in which the #MeToo movement was becoming a witch hunt, a moral panic. Because of women making exaggerated claims, it was "proving to be so over the top" that it had lost "some of its own credibility," becoming so extreme that officemates now feared telling "an attractive associate that they're wearing a nice outfit." Instead of addressing the strength of the overall complaints against Weinstein, he seemed to be using the most strained #MeToo claims to plant the seeds of doubt.

As the backlash developed, others argued that the changes hadn't gone nearly far enough. Social attitudes were shifting, and there were dramatic accusatory headlines almost daily, but the legal and procedural fundamentals were still largely the same. Sexual harassment laws largely were outdated and spottily enforced, and aside from some revisions in a few states, they did not appear likely to change anytime soon. Secret settlements were still being paid—in fact, some lawyers said the dollar amounts were higher than ever—allowing predators to remain hidden. Race and class often had an outsized influence on how cases were handled.

Jodi reported on low-income workers, whose experiences suggested little had shifted structurally. Most of the employers she called, from Walmart to Subway, said their long-standing policies were just fine. Many of the workers she spoke to were inspired and angry: they had watched the actors speak up and felt connected to the experiences of those distant celebrity figures. But they felt unclear about whether they had any avenue for addressing the problem.

Jodi and Megan were hearing all sorts of questions—Who do I contact? What process do I follow?—from numerous women of all backgrounds. The reporters' mobile numbers and email addresses had been passed around, and every day, they were contacted about experiences of harassment, violence, and quiet suffering. On phone calls, women begged Jodi and Megan to investigate their cases, certain that, if they were to write something, it could create some sort of justice.

But there were too many alleged victims of Weinstein, and many other perpetrators, to ever possibly write about. The reporters stumbled trying to explain that the paper was overwhelmed with stories of abuse, that not all could be told, and that even the nation's most powerful publications could not bear the entire weight of the reckoning. Journalists had stepped in when the system failed, but that wasn't a permanent solution.

In a way, those who felt #MeToo had not gone far enough and those who protested that it was going too far were saying some of the same things: there was a lack of process or clear enough rules. The public did not fully agree on the precise meaning of words like "harassment" or "assault," let alone how businesses or schools should investigate or punish them. Everyone from corporate boards to friends chatting in coffee shops seemed to be struggling to develop their own new guidelines, which made for fascinating conversation but also a kind of overall chaos. It was not clear how the country would ever agree on effective new standards or resolve the ocean of outstanding complaints. Instead, the feelings of unfairness on both sides just continued to mount.

During the final months of 2018, Jodi and Megan returned to an idea they had first considered during the Weinstein investigation. Back then, as they struggled to persuade women to break their silence, they wondered if it might help to bring some of them together to talk in person. At the time the idea had seemed impossible, a threat to the essential secrecy of their reporting.

But now they found themselves thinking about the possibility again, for new reasons. They realized it might help answer lingering questions that applied far beyond the Weinstein case: What happened to women who spoke up, and what did they make of everything that had transpired, and the spiraling debates about #MeToo? It was a way to take some measure of the aftermath of their reporting and its impact on the people who had made it possible.

On January 16, 2019, twelve women who had been part of their reporting convened in Los Angeles, at the request of the reporters, to try to answer those questions. Gwyneth Paltrow, who was planning to attend, offered her home in Brentwood. Megan and Jodi paid for the meals so as to avoid accepting anything of substantial financial value from a source. For some participants, travel expenses were a barrier, so they covered a few air tickets and hotel rooms.

Jodi and Megan arrived, along with their sources and subjects, in a heavy rain. Inside, they congregated in the den, which would be their main meeting room for the evening and part of the next day, accepting drinks and settling on wide sofas in front of a crackling fireplace.

Around the room was a history of their reporting, come to life.

Ashley Judd was wearing sweats, because she had come straight from her flight from Germany, where she was living. Since the Weinstein story had been published, she had been praised as a heroine, received awards, and accepted a teaching post at Harvard University's Kennedy School, her alma mater. She was joining the board of Time's Up, the organization to promote safe and fair workplaces that had started in Hollywood in the wake of the Weinstein scandal and spread far beyond it, and had filed her own lawsuit against the producer for harassment, defamation, and loss of career opportunities. Strangers often approached her to convey their gratitude, once even lining up to wait for her as she disembarked from an airplane.

Jodi wanted to see her shake hands with Laura Madden, the former Weinstein assistant with the account of being harassed in Dublin decades ago, who had traveled from Wales. These women didn't know each other, but they were partners, the first two to go on the record about the producer. For all the resolve she had shown in October 2017, Madden remained soft-spoken, tucking her soft brown hair behind her ear, explaining that she was unaccustomed to this type of sharing with strangers.

Madden had flown in with her fellow former Miramax employee Zelda Perkins, who had become an activist. A few weeks after the Weinstein story broke, she had held her breath and become the first of several women to break publicly their settlement nondisclosure agreements, speaking to the press about everything except the specific experience and identity of Rowena Chiu, the colleague she had been trying to protect. In effect, Perkins had dared Weinstein to come after her legally, and he had not. In the media and British Parliament, she had mounted a public case against confidential settlements, questioning the whole notion of hush money to silence accusations of sexual abuse and other wrongdoing.

Walking into Paltrow's house felt strange to her: they had last seen one another working on *Shakespeare in Love* and other films but had never shared with each other their accounts of how Weinstein had behaved. After *Shakespeare in Love* had been released, Paltrow won her Oscar a few months after Perkins had signed the settlement papers that would erase her story for the next twenty years. Now the two blondes were seated side by side on a rug in conversation. Paltrow, still wearing a dress and makeup from a talk show taping, was an easy host, sitting back and letting Megan and Jodi run the proceedings.

In addition to the women Jodi and Megan had named in print, Rowena Chiu joined, standing apart in an important way. Since the Weinstein story had broken, she had remained invisible, communicating with Jodi through her lawyer. She had never been publicly identified or broken her silence and wasn't sure if she ever would. They had invited her to join anyway, not in spite of her silence but because of it: so many women had kept terrible stories to themselves. Maybe Chiu would speak to the consequences of that decision. But she had come on the condition that the group keep her name confidential, if she never decided to come forward, and that her lawyer, Nancy Erika Smith, attend too.

Because Chiu had stayed hidden, Megan and Jodi had imagined her as shy or stricken, but she was warm and confident and had an impressive camera slung over her shoulder. To Jodi's relief, Chiu and her husband were not angry about the awkward moment in the driveway; they understood how confusing the situation had been. She and Perkins had finally been in touch again, trying to figure out who they were to one another after all this time. But Chiu wasn't sure she would speak at the gathering, she warned the reporters. She had still never shared her story out loud with another group of people.

The other women who joined weren't directly related to the Weinstein investigation, but Megan and Jodi had written about them before and after. They too had made the difficult choice to come forward and had seen their personal stories take on a much wider significance.

Kim Lawson was a worker at McDonald's from Kansas City who complained about sexual harassment there and at home, by her landlord. Jodi had first spoken to her almost a year before. Since the *Times* published Jodi's piece describing Lawson's struggles, she had become a leader of the campaign to make the fast food giant, the second-largest employer in the nation, address sexual harassment on the job. She was accompanied by Allynn Umel, an organizer of the labor campaign. But Lawson didn't appear to need any hand-holding: she was vivacious, and judging from the laughter coming from her corner of the room, she seemed to bond quickly with others.

The last participant, Christine Blasey Ford, a psychology professor from California, sat on the couch, flanked by her attorneys, Debra Katz and Lisa Banks. Just a few months earlier, Ford had testified before the Senate Judiciary Committee that Brett Kavanaugh, President Trump's pick for the Supreme Court, had assaulted her at a party during high school. Her accusations were explosive and her testimony emotionally wrenching. Kavanaugh forcefully denied Ford's accusations when it was his turn to speak and ultimately was confirmed for the Supreme Court seat.

It was perhaps the most controversial moment of the #MeToo reckoning, and the reporters had covered it closely: Jodi had shadowed some of Ford's legal team and watched the testimony from the Senate hearing room, and Megan had conducted the first post-hearing interview of Ford. Three months later, Ford was still receiving death threats for speaking out. She hadn't even returned to local shopping for fear of being approached by strangers, let alone to the teaching job she loved. But she had told Megan that coming to Los Angeles reflected her new determination to venture out.

Rachel Crooks, who during the 2016 presidential campaign had told Megan her account of being forcibly kissed by Donald Trump at a Trump Tower elevator, had traveled from Ohio, where she was still dealing with the fallout of sharing her story. The *Times* had published that piece by Megan and Michael Barbaro two years earlier. It had brought Crooks more opportunities—and more problems—than she had ever imagined. Seeing the tall Midwesterner in the California home was jolting to Megan—but perhaps no more than everything else that had happened since the two had first spoken.

Beginning to mingle, the women were friendly but tentative. Almost all were strangers to one another, and the thing they had in common was so unusual. Each had obsessed over the decision to share her account of harassment or assault, in many cases with either Jodi or Megan coaxing and encouraging them on the other end of the phone. They had asked the women to come to the gathering prepared to answer one central question: After the leap of faith, what had they found on the other side?

Jodi and Megan made a quick round of introductions, explaining the role that each person had played in their journalism, and soon everyone was settling in at a long table with plates of Japanese food—skewers, salads, rice. The women went around the table, each saying something about how she had decided to speak up, and the conversation began to warm up. During Paltrow's turn, she raised a glass and toasted Judd for being the first actress to break the silence about Weinstein.

"Ashley, honestly, what you did—it's very, very hard to be first into the breach," she said, acknowledging that in speaking on the record in the first Weinstein story, Judd had gone where she had not. "You really were the one who paved the way for all of us to come forward in your wake," she said.

"I always worried about you," Judd said back to her—meaning back in the '90s and whether she was safe from Weinstein.

As the conversation went around the table, some common experiences began to surface. Crooks explained that some of her own family members supported Trump, not her. Perkins said that for all the public attention she had received for her battle against secret settlements, some relatives had never once acknowledged her efforts. Madden said that she had been able to speak out about Weinstein in part because she was confident her encounters with him were part of a broader predatory pattern.

When it was Chiu's turn, Jodi gave her an out, asking if she wanted to pass.

"Sure, I will take a turn," she said—brief words, but for her, momentous ones. "I'm the only person at the table who has not yet gone public with my story, so I've had very little practice in telling it," Chiu said. Aside from her husband, her family still knew nothing, she said.

"There are very few, I feel, Asian voices that come forward with this kind of story," she continued. "It's not because this kind of thing does not happen to Asian people, but I think certainly within the US we have a whole culture around a model minority that doesn't make a fuss, that doesn't speak up, that puts their head down and works really hard and doesn't cause waves."

For those reasons and others, Chiu said, she was now contemplating breaking her silence. "The whole idea of coming out and speaking about something that would undoubtedly shock my friends, and shift the whole of my life, is really terrifying," she said. "It's really helpful to be here tonight to hear each of your perspectives, especially about how you've come forward and what made you come forward."

With that, the agenda became more urgent and concrete. For Jodi and Megan, this gathering was an interview to share with readers. For Chiu, it was potential help in making a life-defining choice.

Chiu gestured to her camera and asked if she could take some shots that night and the next day. She had given herself a perfect job: she could hide behind the lens, remaining invisible if she preferred, observing everyone else.

The group reassembled the next morning, forming a loose circle on the same couches and chairs in the den. At the center, a huge gray-and-white ottoman held cups of coffee—and flowerpots containing microphones. This was still an interview, and Megan and Jodi were recording, as everyone knew. The plan for the next few hours was simple: they asked the women to take turns sharing stories about what happened after they came forward and hoped the conversation would build from there. Outside, it was still raining, adding to a sense of refuge.

Laura Madden was still nervous about speaking. She was modest, and she had gotten relatively little credit for her bravery, continuing to rinse dishes and supervise homework in Swansea. But in her lilting accent, she told the other women what had happened, simply in her own head, in the wake of the Weinstein story: she had rewritten the history of her adult life. No one could restore the years Madden, now forty-eight, had spent feeling uneasy about her time at Miramax or hand her a fresh career or financial success. But "just being able to see it as his problem has helped get some sense of myself back," she said.

Paltrow, sitting cross-legged on the rug by the warmth of the fireplace, described a very different kind of change in understanding her personal history and career. After the story had broken of Weinstein's misconduct, she learned that the producer had used her—her name, her Oscar, her success—as a means of manipulating other vulnerable women. Starting in the fall of 2017, Paltrow had spent many hours on the phone with other women who told her that Weinstein, while harassing or assaulting them, would routinely cite her and her soaring career, falsely implying she had yielded to him. "He was pointing to my career and saying, 'Don't you want what she has?'"

Weinstein denied he had ever made those claims about Paltrow, but it seemed this was why he had been so worried about the prospect of her speaking up: once others knew her story, his scheme would fall apart. Paltrow spoke through tears. "It almost makes me feel culpable in some way, even though it's completely illogical." As she spoke, her home's luxury suddenly looked a little different: Weinstein had taken Paltrow's enviable life and deployed it against other women.

As each woman spoke, the others focused intently, with few phone checks and no interruptions. Each one was a messenger from an unfamiliar world: the battleground Midwest; show business; the thunder dome of Supreme Court confirmation hearings. Those differences, rather than splitting the group, generated curiosity and drew the women together.

Perkins described how she had felt delivering testimony about confidentiality agreements to members of Parliament: "The most extraordinary thing for me was walking into the Palace at Westminster and realizing that as an individual, that this was actually mine—the Palace at Westminster was mine, the politicians were mine."

Their stories involved a kind of poetic reversal. They had suffered from harassment but gained new authority and respect from fighting it. Lawson had become a kind of team coach to other female McDonald's employees across the country involved in the union push, counseling them on a text chain. Customers looked at her differently: "Weren't you on TV about sexual harassment?" they asked her.

"Since I've spoken I've been able to come into the person that I was growing into at twenty-four," Perkins said, citing the age she had been when she left Miramax.

But neither Perkins nor Lawson could report complete triumphs. Settlement laws had not changed in the UK, and Perkins did not know if they would. McDonald's was beginning to strengthen its policies, introducing new training for managers and a hotline, and making plans for posters giving employees instructions on how to report. But Lawson hadn't yet seen any of those changes materialize in her own store, and it was not yet clear how much the company's thousands of workplaces would shift.

"There's a huge part of me that can't wait for it all to be over and then to just go back to my horses, and my sheep, and never ever have to speak to a journalist, or be on TV, or do any of those things ever again," Perkins said.

Some of the women nodded. Together, they had all been part of a genuine realignment, but it was so incomplete. How much more of themselves did each want to donate to the effort?

After Rachel Crooks came forward about Trump in 2016, she suffered from crippling anxiety and self-consciousness, she said as she sat facing the others with her long legs tucked beneath her. She was the only one present who lived in a rural, conservative area—"more of a #himtoo community," as she called it.

Even so, she made the decision to run for a seat in the state legislature in 2018 because she cared about education and health care. She lost her race but didn't feel self-pity: Democrats had, for the most part, lost across Ohio. But months later, she was struggling with the tendency of others to continue to view her only through her Trump story.

The group silently considered her dilemma. Crooks was living out one of the most common fears about coming forward: it could label you forever. Ford listened particularly closely. Her current fears matched what Crooks described having faced two years before, right down to a specific detail about avoiding local stores. Sitting on the couch, with her red glasses pushed up on her head, she began quizzing Crooks, as if she held a map to what lay ahead.

"I was wondering how long that lasted before you just sort of normally jump into your car and go to a restaurant without people looking at you and wondering if that's really you," Ford said. She was also struggling online, including with fake social media profiles of herself saying, "I recant my whole story."

"I'm like, 'That's not true!'" Ford said. "But I'm not brave enough to get into that with them. And there's just too many of them, so . . . the social media piece . . . I don't do well with that," she said.

"Sometimes I write the replies and I just never post them," Crooks told her. "It's very cathartic."

The reaction wasn't all negative, Ford acknowledged. She had been offered prizes, invitations, book and movie contracts. The mail for her was still accumulating, including many private stories of violence—"175,000 letters in Palo Alto," Katz interjected. Those were only the paper letters.

There were many more electronic missives. In those, and everywhere else, the reactions to what she had done were so extreme, generating alternating currents of praise and blame.

For hours, the others had mostly been nodding and asking polite follow-up questions. Now they spoke up with purpose. Paltrow and Judd—longtime experts in fielding public scrutiny and criticism—began to coach everyone else in how to deal with other people's judgments. Judd was direct: stop reading about yourself online.

"If an alcoholic can stay away from a drink one day at a time, I can stay away from the comment section one day at a time," Judd said. "I'm participating in my own self-harm when I expose myself to that material," she continued.

"Do you just not really go on the internet much?" Ford asked Judd, incredulous.

"I'm completely abstinent from all media about myself and have been for probably almost twenty years," Judd said. She posted pictures and links on social media but tried not to read anything written about herself: that was part of why she had disappeared to the woods after the first Weinstein article had been published.

As she spoke, she was curled in a pink upholstered chair facing the group. She had sat there all day, absorbing what others had to say, speaking relatively little. She seemed like the one participant who had not really been transformed. She had always wanted to be an activist, and when she went on the record about Weinstein, the world affirmed her instincts.

"I have to know the hill on which I'm willing to die," she told the group. "The equality of the sexes is that hill for me."

Throughout the discussion, Chiu sat listening, saying little, occasionally clicking her camera in the direction of the others. No one pressed her on the momentous decision of whether she would say publicly what had happened to her all those years ago.

But during the final hours of the gathering, as Ford spoke more, Chiu seemed to hang on every word. Ford had become, in Chiu's mind, a kind of proxy for what she might undergo if she went public, she told the group. The fact that the two women turned out to be neighbors only heightened the connection she felt. Even as Chiu kept her story hidden, she watched as friends and neighbors had organized a candlelight vigil and meal deliveries for Ford.

For months, Chiu had pictured the controversy and criticism that engulfed Ford happening to her instead. The analogy was inexact—the Weinstein case was far more settled and less controversial—but for her, it was real. "I imagined it would all come crashing down," Chiu admitted to the rest of the group. "There'd be news vans outside my door. I was worried my children would be followed to school."

That mental exercise was having an unexpected effect. Watching Ford from nearby—and now meeting her up close—had strengthened

Chiu's desire to go public. She told the group that she could feel herself getting closer to joining them, to putting her name to her story. "I can't say that being in this room with so many of you—I can't say that doesn't inspire me," she said.

"I think it's really going to change who I am," she added. That had turned out to be the strongest unifying thread after the hours of discussion: almost every member of the group who had spoken publicly had been transformed by it, and was stunned by the impact that sharing her own intimate story had on others.

The women around the room leaped in with expressions of support. "If you decide to come forward, that's a big step and that's a step of growth," Lawson said. "No matter how long it took you to say anything about it."

"If you do it, we have your back," Paltrow said.

No one could ever predict how speaking out would go. Forecasting was futile. Once a story was publicly told for the first time, there was no telling what might happen, who might read it, or what others might echo, add, or disagree with. There was no guarantee of affirmation or impact. The results could be wrenching, empowering, or both.

But this was what everyone in the room, and more people beyond it, now understood: if the story was not shared, nothing would change. Problems that are not seen cannot be addressed. In the world of journalism, the story was the end, the result, the final product. But in the world at large, the emergence of new information was just the beginning—of conversation, action, change.

"We're still here," Perkins said, to laughter, in one of the group's final exchanges. She wasn't speaking directly to Chiu, but the message was clear. "We're still smiling. None of us died from stepping forward. We walked through the fire, but we all came out the other side."

A few weeks later, Chiu called: she was ready to go on the record, and for Megan and Jodi to share her name publicly.

She understood that more than eighty women had already come forward about Weinstein. She wasn't sure that the public would still care about her account. But she wanted to speak anyway. During the initial Weinstein investigation, she hadn't been ready, but the other women, in Los Angeles and around the world, had eased the way. She feared the legal cases against him might not be successful. So she wanted to help write the history and continue pushing for change.

"I'm not just going to let it slide away," she said.

EPILOGUE

ON A LATE morning in February of 2020, almost exactly a year after the gathering in Los Angeles, the original team that worked on the Harvey Weinstein investigation rushed to reassemble in the newsroom. Rebecca Corbett, Dean Baquet, and Matt Purdy hovered behind Jodi and Megan, who sat side by side. The jury in the Harvey Weinstein trial in New York was about to deliver a verdict.

The group of journalists had no idea what to expect.

Jodi and Megan had been reporting on the criminal case in New York for months, observing at every turn that it was much more complicated than many people realized. The two women at the center of the case acknowledged having consensual sex with Weinstein after the alleged attacks, and had maintained friendly contact with him for years. The reporters knew such behavior was common—there was almost no "perfect" rape victim, and both women had professional reasons to keep in touch with the producer. But Jodi and Megan also learned that complex cases like that were almost never prosecuted. Law enforcement officials assumed that juries would find them too messy to convict.

Weinstein had seized on the complicating factors to mount a fierce and sweeping defense. He and his lawyers argued that the women and other witnesses had actually been manipulating him for professional advantage. They continued to insist that case was proof that the entire #MeToo movement had gone too far. In an interview with Megan, one of the lawyers, Donna Rotunno, who had made her career representing men accused of sexual misconduct, said she had never been the victim of sexual assault "because I would never put myself in that position," insinuating that even when attacks did happen, the victims were responsible.

So as Jodi and Megan sat next to one another, passing the long minutes until the verdict was announced, they knew what was at stake. Even though the trial was too narrow to be a true test of the movement, because it rested on just a few women's stories, it was being seen that way around the world. If Weinstein was declared not guilty, what would that mean for the social shift that had ensued? They felt confident that their journalism would last no matter the outcome, but were also aware that if he was acquitted, journalism might be one of the only forms of accountability Weinstein might ever face.

Then they heard the word "guilty." Twice. Weinstein had been convicted of raping both women, acquitted of some other charges, and sent straight to jail to await sentencing. Prosecutors had pushed the boundaries of which victims of sex crimes are entitled to criminal justice, and they had won. The jury had believed the women and had ruled for them. The cultural change that had started with the newspaper was making its way into the courtroom.

Jodi and Megan exchanged a deep glance, alone with one another for a moment in the crowded newsroom.

Then they got to work. They had sources to call for their reactions, stories to write. Their colleagues were already polishing, posting. This wasn't a slow, deliberate investigation, but breaking news that had to be conveyed as quickly and accurately as possible.

Jodi phoned Ashley Judd to tell her the three-minute-old news personally. They had shared so many consequential phone calls over the previous three years, and this felt like the final one in the set. Judd, deliberate as usual, let it all sink in. What she had helped start. Where it was ending.

"The story of #MeToo, of what the movement is about, is that men no longer have tacit permission to use their power or prestige to sexually access girls' and women's bodies," Judd said. "There will be consequences in the courtroom, in employment, and in society."

Next, Jodi phoned Irwin Reiter, who seemed stunned that his former boss was facing long-term imprisonment. "The guy thought he could do whatever he wanted," he said. "Everyone who worked for him heard it a thousand times: 'I'm Superman and you're not. I'm a genius and you're all clerks.'" A colleague called Rowena Chiu, who had become a confident narrator of her own story, giving interviews and taking pride in what she had overcome. "In some ways, I feel that the life I've built today, every day that I live and enjoy my life, is a victory over Harvey," she said.

A few weeks later, Jodi and Megan sat in the courtroom, just a few feet behind Weinstein himself. While the verdict from three weeks back had established his guilt, this hearing would determine his sentence, the punishment he'd face. The benches were crammed, and Jodi and Megan had only gotten in at the last minute. Because almost no one had turned up to support Weinstein, they had been given two of the seats allotted for his friends and family.

The six victims who had testified sat in the first row, clutching one another, a few of them delivering stirring statements. Reiter was a few rows away, and so was Lance Maerov. Gloria Allred was there too; despite the recent scrutiny of her and her daughter, Lisa Bloom, she was still being hired, and one of the witnesses who had testified against Weinstein was a client.

And in the front of the court was Weinstein, confined to a wheel-chair because he was recovering from back surgery. He gave a long, rambling, somewhat apologetic but self-flattering monologue.

Then the judge slammed down one of the lengthiest sentences possible: twenty-three years in prison. Weinstein was already sixty-seven. He would likely spend the rest of his life behind bars.

"Although this is a first conviction, it is not a first offense," the judge said.

The Weinstein saga had finally come to a clear, irreversible ending. Breaking the story had opened the floodgates. The ensuing #MeToo wave had rushed through, untidy and wild, but also forceful, galvaniz-ing, and clarifying. And now the criminal justice system had shown a heightened commitment to protecting victims.

The courtroom was the last stop in a through line: from the women who mustered the courage to break their silence, to the work of inves-tigative journalists who chased the truth, to a report that was airtight and unassailable and nurtured by an institution devoted to questioning the mighty, the *New York Times*. That line extended even further back, to the system designed by America's founders, to the First Amendment, which protects the public's right to confront abuses of power.

This was the work that Jodi and Megan felt honored to do. This was the enduring power of the press.

ACKNOWLEDGMENTS

If you've read these pages, you already have some sense of the debts we owe. Those are only the beginning.

To all of our sources: thank you for participating in our journalism. Some of you spoke with us at great personal risk or confided stories you never thought you would share with a stranger—and then shared even more for this book. Many of you submitted to lengthy, repeated questioning or uncomfortable lines of inquiry. A special measure of gratitude to everyone who provided the illuminating emails, texts, and other documents interspersed throughout this narrative. A much larger cast, from experts to silent tipsters we can never name, provided essential guidance, including stories and ideas that ring in our heads still.

In addition to the colleagues portrayed in this book, we're grateful to the *Times* journalists who joined our efforts on the Weinstein story, including Rachel Abrams, Ellen Gabler, Susan Dominus, Steve Eder, Jim Rutenberg, William Rashbaum, Barry Meier, Al Baker, Jim McKinley, and the audio team at *The Daily*. At every turn, we received crucial support from Arthur Sulzberger Jr., A. G. Sulzberger, Sam

Dolnick, our colleagues on the business side of the newspaper, and from subscribers, who make this journalism possible. Dean Baquet, Matt Purdy, David McCraw, Sheryl Stolberg, Emily Steel, Carolyn Ryan, and Michael Barbaro generously provided feedback on the manuscript.

The editor who is invisible in this book yet present on every page is Ann Godoff, our galvanizing force. Ann endowed this project with her vision, clarity, and decisiveness, and notes so inspiring we hung them on our office walls. For all of that, we are forever grateful. William Heyward and Casey Denis, Sarah Hutson and Gail Brussel, Carolyn Foley and Juliann Barbato all poured many hours and years of experience into helping us tell and share this story. Thank you for your extraordinary dedication.

Rebecca Corbett, our editor at the *Times*, is our true north. She not only steered us through our investigation of Weinstein but also read and commented on several versions of these chapters, helping us capture and explain what we witnessed.

From the beginning, we hoped *She Said* would reach students, aspiring journalists, and those entering the profession. So we were thrilled when Jill Santopolo proposed that we turn the original book into this version, specifically for those readers. Thank you, Jill, for this special chance. Ruby Shamir adapted the book with sensitivity and insight, seeing every page with new eyes, and somehow made the process easy, even during pandemic conditions. Thanks also to Cheryl Eissing, Elise Poston and Gerard Mancini in managing editorial, copyeditors Marinda Valenti and Kate Frentzel, designer Ellice Lee, cover designer Kelley Brady, publisher Ken Wright, Elyse Marshall and Anna Elling in publicity, the Trade, Digital, and School and Library marketing teams, and everyone else at Philomel Books who helped create *Chasing the Truth*. We were also aided by a sharp-eyed squad of journalism students from the Packer Collegiate Institute, whose comments further improved the revised manuscript: John Benson, Daniel Biro, Meleana Buice, Violet Chernoff, Lily Crowell, Apple Diamond, Madeleine Farr, Sophie Germain, Maya Gomes, Julian Hartman-Sigall, Kayla Johnson, Amaya Joseph, Amelia Killackey, Sage Lewit, Liam Wilson Mackenzie, Natalie Marcus-Wade, Antonio Mota, Carly Mraz, Zola Narisetti, Caroline Peyser, Leo Raykher, Abe M. Rothstein, Charlie Susser, Audrey Taplitz, Sandy Tecotzky, Chloe Vincent, and Sylvan Wold. We hope you become investigative journalists, but you're already very good editors.

Alexis Kirschbaum, our editor and ally in London, provided essential insight, feedback, and friendship. Thank you as well to Emma Bal and Jasmine Horsey of Bloomsbury Publishing.

Elyse Cheney is our agent, matchmaker, and guide, and we are grateful for her tenacity, judgment, and hustle. We're also indebted to her colleagues Claire Gillespie, Alice Whitwham, Alex Jacobs, and Allison Devereux. Charlotte Perman and Kristen Sena of Greater Talent Network have handled our speaking engagements with grace—particularly the campus visits, with questions from students that helped us articulate what we wanted to say in these pages.

Kelsey Kudak fact-checked the manuscript with sensitivity and commitment, moving through hundreds of pages of complicated investigative work and taking direction from two different authors with equanimity. Astha Rajvanshi provided research assistance on topics large and small.

For other essential help, we'd also like to thank Joseph Abboud, Kendra Barkoff, Kassie Evashevski, Natasha Fairweather, Jonathan Furmanski, Molly Levinson, Eleanor Leonard, Priya Parker, Melissa Schwartz, Felicia Stewart, Nancy Erika Smith, and Josh Wilkinson. For our author photos, we were lucky enough to have a photographer who knows a thing or two about portraits in the extended *She Said* family; many thanks to Martin Schoeller and his team for these pictures.

Anyone who has parented young children can instantly fill in the scenes of diaper-changing, bottle-feeding, and sleep-training that took place in between (and occasionally during) our reporting. We were saved again and again by our babysitters, our children's teachers, and most of all, our families.

From Jodi: not everything in life happens in the order you expect. During the period described in this book, I needed my parents, Wendy and Harry Kantor, more than I have at any time since childhood, because of the constancy of their love and the way they frequently swept in to care for, entertain, and guide my own children. Mom and Dad; Charlene Lieber, my second mother; calm, brave Fred Lieber; and the entire extended Kantor Lieber clan: thank you for seeing us through these frantic years. Donna Mitchell, thank you for being a force of calm and goodness in the lives of our daughters, and for sharing the biggest and smallest moments with us.

Ron: even as you unearthed stories of financial wrongdoing and reported on your own book on what to pay for college, you backed this work with full force, encouraging, feeding, and sustaining me. One of the best gifts you ever gave me was the Post-it you left on my desk, a few days before the publication of the original Weinstein story, that read, "You can do this." Yes, but only with your love, help, and devotion.

Talia, you are a light, a lockbox, and an increasingly formidable discussion partner and debater. You overheard things that no tween should hear, faithfully kept secrets, helped with your little sister, and kept your cool even as I was often absorbed in broader dramas. Watching you articulate who you really are, and begin to build a life, is the thrill of mine.

Violet, you were only a year and a half old when we started, and your innocence made you my refuge. Parents are supposed to console their children, but I frequently found solace in your curls, songs, made-up words, discoveries, and above all, in the fierceness of your embrace.

From Megan: I'm indebted to my parents, John and Mary Jane Twohey, who have served as my moral compass for decades, reinforcing my values, nudging me along the pursuit of truth, and picking me up whenever I stumble. Ben and Maya Rutman, Helen and Felix Rutman-Schoeller, and Martin Schoeller, I am thankful for your endless kindness and joyous laughter. Jenny Rattan-John, you are our rock, our teacher, and a cherished member of our family.

Jim: we had been married for less than a year and were brand-new parents when the Weinstein investigation began. Not once did you teeter in your support of the project and later this book, even when it meant canceled vacations, long stretches of single parenting, and fielding the intense emotions that came with this work. Your warm hugs, sharp listening skills, and encouraging texts propelled me forward, and your own expertise and judgment as a literary agent were delivered up at just the right moments.

Mira: you learned how to walk and talk during the course of this reporting, and the feistiness with which you tackled each stage of development served as a major source of inspiration. I am increasingly impressed by and grateful for your grit, cunning, and passion.

To our daughters, and to yours: may you know respect and dignity always, in the workplace and beyond.

NOTES

This book is based on three years of our reporting, stretching from the spring of 2017 through the spring of 2020, with a focus on Harvey Weinstein's decades of alleged sexual harassment and abuse. These notes are intended to provide readers with a road map of which information in this book came from which sources.

We conducted hundreds of interviews, speaking with almost everyone depicted in this book. Bob Weinstein, David Boies, Lance Maerov, Irwin Reiter, and most of the alleged victims portrayed granted us multiple interviews. Some of what we share was originally off the record, such as Jodi's early conversations with Reiter, and Weinstein's October 4, 2017, surprise visit to the *Times*, but through additional reporting, including returning to the parties involved, we were able to include the material. Over the past two years, we have sought comment from Weinstein on our findings multiple times, most recently in spring 2019. Kelsey Kudak spent five months fact-checking the book, often adding new information.

We reviewed thousands of pages of documents, cited below,

including internal records from The Weinstein Company. Some text messages, emails, and other primary records are reproduced in the book so that readers can examine them directly.

We also drew on the reporting of other journalists, including Ronan Farrow, Emily Steel, and Michael Schmidt.

CHAPTER ONE: THE FIRST PHONE CALL

"Here's the thing, I have been treated": Rose McGowan, email message to Jodi Kantor, May 11, 2017.

McGowan had accused an unnamed producer—rumored to be Weinstein: Rose McGowan (@rosemcgowan), Twitter, October 13, 2016, twitter.com/rosemcgowan/status/786723360550035460.

writing a memoir: Rose McGowan, *Brave* (New York: HarperCollins, 2018).

"tank that shows off cleavage (push-up bras encouraged)": Rose McGowan (@rosemcgowan), "casting note that came w/script I got today. For real. name of male star rhymes with Madam Panhandler hahahaha I die," Twitter, June 17, 2015, twitter.com/rosemcgowan/status/611378426344288256.

"It is okay to be angry": Rose McGowan (@rosemcgowan), "It is okay to be angry. Don't be afraid of it. Lean in. Like a storm cloud it passes, but it must be recognized. #readthis," Twitter, April 3, 2017, twitter.com/rosemcgowan/status/849083550448193536; "dismantle the system," Twitter, May 4, 2017, twitter.com/rosemcgowan/status/860322650962264064.

"At some pt": Jennifer Senior (@JenSeniorNY), "At some pt, all the women who've been afraid to speak out abt Harvey Weinstein are gonna have to hold hands and jump," Twitter, March 30, 2015, twitter.com/jenseniorny/status/582657086737289216.

about a horrific sexual assault: Sabrina Rubin Erdely, "A Rape on Campus," *Rolling Stone*, November 4, 2014. *Rolling Stone* retracted the story on April 5, 2015, and commissioned a study by the *Columbia Journalism Review*, which was published by the magazine. Sheila Coronel, Steve Coll, and Derek Kravitz, *"Rolling Stone* and UVA: The Columbia University Graduate School of Journalism Report," *Rolling Stone*, April 5, 2015, rollingstone.com/culture/culture-news/rolling-stone-and-uva-the-columbia-university-graduate-school-of-journalism-report-44930; Ravi Somaiya, *"Rolling Stone* Article on Rape at University of Virginia Failed All Basics, Report Says," *The New York Times*, April 5, 2015, nytimes.com/2015/04/06/business/media/rolling-stone-retracts-article-on-rape-at-university-of-virginia.html.

a series of lawsuits: Ben Sisario, Hawes Spencer, and Sydney Ember, *"Rolling Stone* Loses Defamation Case over Rape Story," *The New York Times*, November 4, 2016, nytimes.com/2016/11/05/business/media/rolling-stone-rape-story-case-guilty.html; Hawes Spencer and Ben Sisario, "In *Rolling Stone* Defamation Case, Magazine and Reporter Ordered to Pay $3 Million," *The New York Times*, November 7, 2016, nytimes.com/2016/11/08/business/media/in-rolling-stone-defamation-case-magazine-and-reporter-ordered-to-pay-3-million.html; Matthew Haag, *"Rolling Stone* Settles Lawsuit over Debunked Campus Rape Article," *The New York Times*, April 11, 2017, nytimes.com/2017/04/11/business/

media/rolling-stone-university-virginia-rape-story-settlement.html; Sydney Ember, *"Rolling Stone* to Pay $1.65 Million to Fraternity over Discredited Rape Story," *The New York Times,* June 13, 2017, nytimes.com/2017/06/13/business/media/rape-uva-rolling-stone-frat.html.

police had called the story "a complete crock": Erik Wemple, "Charlottesville Police Make Clear That *Rolling Stone* Story Is a Complete Crock," *The Washington Post,* March 23, 2015, washingtonpost.com/blogs/erik-wemple/wp/2015/03/23/charlottesville-police-make-clear-that-rolling-stone-story-is-a-complete-crock; Bill Grueskin, "More Is Not Always Better," *Columbia Journalism Review,* April 5, 2015, cjr.org/analysis/rolling_stone_journalism.php; Craig Silverman, "The Year in Media Errors and Corrections 2014," Poynter Institute, December 18, 2014, poynter.org/newsletters/2014/the-year-in-media-errors-and-corrections-2014.

many women's accounts were told in their own words: Michael Barbaro and Megan Twohey, "Crossing the Line: How Donald Trump Behaved with Women in Private," *The New York Times,* May 14, 2016, nytimes.com/2016/05/15/us/politics/donald-trump-women.html.

conducted a lengthy interview of the candidate: Donald Trump, interview by Megan Twohey and Michael Barbaro, May 10, 2016.

His argument was absurd: Erik Wemple, "Bill O'Reilly Follows Donald Trump into the Racist Hellhole," *The Washington Post,* June 7, 2016, washingtonpost.com/blogs/erik-wemple/wp/2016/06/07/bill-oreilly-follows-donald-trump-into-racist-hellhole.

two women who accused Trump: Megan Twohey and Michael Barbaro, "Two Women Say Donald Trump Touched Them Inappropriately," *The New York Times,* October 12, 2016, nytimes.com/2016/10/13/us/politics/donald-trump-women.html.

"He seethed on the line": Donald Trump, interview by Megan Twohey, October 11, 2016.

Trump's lawyer sent a letter to Baquet: Marc Kasowitz, "re: Demand for Retraction," letter from Marc Kasowitz to David McCraw, October 12, 2016, assets.donaldjtrump.com/DemandForRetraction.PDF.

"It would have been a disservice": David McCraw, "re: Demand for Retraction," letter from David McCraw to Marc Kasowitz, October 13, 2016, nytimes.com/interactive/2016/10/13/us/politics/david-mccraw-trump-letter.html.

had covered up repeated allegations: Emily Steel and Michael S. Schmidt, "Bill O'Reilly Thrives at Fox News, Even as Harassment Settlements Add Up," *The New York Times,* April 1, 2017, nytimes.com/2017/04/01/business/media/bill-oreilly-sexual-harassment-fox-news.html.

big companies like Mercedes-Benz: Karl Russel, "Bill O'Reilly's Show Lost More Than Half Its Advertisers in a Week," *The New York Times,* April 11, 2017, nytimes.com/interactive/2017/04/11/business/oreilly-advertisers.html.

other women at Fox started: Emily Steel and Michael S. Schmidt, "Bill O'Reilly Is Forced Out at Fox News," *The New York Times,* April 19, 2017, nytimes.com/2017/04/19/business/media/bill-oreilly-fox-news-allegations.html.

Roger Ailes, the Republican power broker: John Koblin and Jim Rutenberg, "Accused of Sexual Harassment, Roger Ailes Is Negotiating Exit from Fox," *The New York Times,* July 19, 2016, nytimes.com/2016/07/20/business/media/roger-ailes-fox-news-murdoch.html.

Shaunna Thomas, a feminist activist: Shaunna Thomas, interview by Jodi Kantor, April 2017.

CHAPTER TWO: HOLLYWOOD SECRETS

red-carpet photos: "2017 Cannes Film Festival Red Carpet Looks," photos, *The New York Times*, May 20, 2017, nytimes.com/2017/05/20/fashion/2017-cannes-film-festival-red-carpet-looks.html.

given an interview to *Variety* in 2015: Ramin Setoodeh, "Ashley Judd Reveals Harassment by Studio Mogul," *Variety*, October 6, 2015, variety.com/2015/film/news/ashley-judd-sexual-harassment-studio-mogul-shower-1201610666.

"I am so sorry, my lawyer": Judith Godrèche, email message to Jodi Kantor, June 13, 2017.

wasn't a Weinstein victim: Marisa Tomei, interviews by Jodi Kantor, 2017–18.

a gushing tweet a few months before: Lisa Bloom (@LisaBloom), "BIG ANNOUNCEMENT: My book SUSPICION NATION is being made into a miniseries, produced by Harvey Weinstein and Jay Z!," Twitter, April 7, 2017, twitter.com/lisabloom/status/850402622116855809.

made getting in touch with Ashley Judd simple: Ashley Judd and Maryanne Vollers, *All That Is Bitter and Sweet* (New York: Ballantine, 2015).

she had a personal story to tell: Ashley Judd, interviews by Jodi Kantor and Megan Twohey, June 2017–January 2019.

Loneliness had defined Ashley Judd's upbringing: many of the details of Judd's upbringing are chronicled in her 2015 autobiography, Judd and Vollers, *All That Is Bitter and Sweet*.

Professor Diane Rosenfeld: Diane Rosenfeld, interview by Jodi Kantor, May 11, 2018.

"I propose a model": Ashley Judd, "Gender Violence: Law and Social Justice" (master's thesis, Harvard's Kennedy School of Government), 2010.

Jenni Konner: Jenni Konner, interviews by Jodi Kantor, 2017; Lena Dunham, interviews by Jodi Kantor, 2017.

Paltrow shared the unknown side of the story: Gwyneth Paltrow, interviews by Jodi Kantor and Megan Twohey, 2017–19.

the producer's mother: Anita Gates, "Miriam Weinstein, Mother and Backbone of Original Miramax, Dies at 90," *The New York Times*, November 4, 2016, nytimes.com/2016/11/04/movies/miriam-weinstein-died-miramax.html.

She did not reply: Uma Thurman, interviews and emails with Jodi Kantor, 2017–19.

While reporting on a different story: Linda Fairstein, interview by Megan Twohey, conducted in 2009 while reporting at the *Chicago Tribune*.

liked to boast of his coziness with media: Ryan Tate, "Why Harvey Weinstein Thinks He Owns New York Media," Gawker, April 2, 2008, gawker.com/5004915/why-harvey-weinstein-thinks-he-owns-new-york-media.

CHAPTER THREE: HOW TO SILENCE A VICTIM

the corresponding state agencies: the New York Division of Human Rights, dhr.ny.gov, and the California Department of Fair Employment and Housing, dfeh.ca.gov.

obtained a report: generated in 2017 by the California Department of Fair Employment and Housing.

On the afternoon of July 14: meeting notes and documents from Katie Benner and Jodi Kantor.

Two weeks before, Katie Benner: Katie Benner, "Women in Tech Speak Frankly on Culture of Harassment," *The New York Times*, June 30, 2017, nytimes.com/

2017/06/30/technology/women-entrepreneurs-speak-out-sexual-harassment.
html.
One of the men and one of the firms: Katie Benner, "A Backlash Builds against Sexual
Harassment in Silicon Valley," *The New York Times*, July 3, 2017, nytimes.
com/2017/07/03/technology/silicon-valley-sexual-harassment.html.
Steel was hearing alarming accounts: Emily Steel, "At *Vice*, Cutting-Edge Media and
Allegations of Old-School Sexual Harassment," *The New York Times*, December
23, 2017, nytimes.com/2017/12/23/business/media/vice-sexual-harassment.
html.
conversations with restaurant, retail, hotel, and construction workers: Catrin Einhorn,
"Harassment and Tipping in Restaurants: Your Stories," *The New York Times*,
March 18, 2018, nytimes.com/2018/03/18/business/restaurant-harassment-
tipping.html; Catrin Einhorn and Rachel Abrams, "The Tipping Equation," *The
New York Times*, March 12, 2018, nytimes.com/interactive/2018/03/11/business/
tipping-sexual-harassment.html.
male-dominated workplaces: Susan Chira and Catrin Einhorn, "How Tough Is It to
Change a Culture of Harassment? Ask Women at Ford," *The New York Times*,
December 19, 2017, nytimes.com/interactive/2017/12/19/us/ford-chicago-
sexual-harassment.html; Susan Chira and Catrin Einhorn, "The #MeToo
Moment: Blue-collar Women Ask, 'What About Us?'" *The New York Times*,
December 20, 2017, nytimes.com/2017/12/20/us/the-metoo-moment-blue-
collar-women-ask-what-about-us.html; Susan Chira, "We Asked Women in
Blue-collar Workplaces about Sexual Harassment: Here Are Their Stories," *The
New York Times*, December 29, 2017, nytimes.com/2017/12/29/us/blue-collar-
women-harassment.html; Susan Chira, "The 'Manly' Jobs Problem," *The New
York Times*, February 8, 2018, nytimes.com/2018/02/08/sunday-review/sexual-
harassment-masculine-jobs.html.
If they received subpoenas: Emily Steel, "How Bill O'Reilly Silenced His Accusers," *The
New York Times*, April 4, 2018, nytimes.com/2018/04/04/business/media/how-
bill-oreilly-silenced-his-accusers.html.
Even the EEOC: Chai Feldblum, interview by Jodi Kantor, May 11, 2017.
given up control of Miramax, their first movie company: after selling Miramax to
Disney for $80 million in 1993, the Weinsteins separated themselves from Disney
in 2005. Laura M. Holson, "How the Tumultuous Marriage of Miramax and
Disney Failed," *The New York Times*, March 6, 2005, nytimes.com/2005/03/06/
movies/how-the-tumultuous-marriage-of-miramax-and-disney-failed.html.
to the home of John Schmidt: John Schmidt, interviews by Megan Twohey, September
2017–spring 2019.
One Friday evening: Amy Israel, interviews by Jodi Kantor, 2017–19.
A few weeks later: Zelda Perkins, interviews by Jodi Kantor, 2017–19.
Much later, Chiu told Jodi: Rowena Chiu, interviews by Jodi Kantor, May–June 2019.
With a more senior producer: Donna Gigliotti, emails to Jodi Kantor and Kelsey Kudak,
November 2017–June 2019.
driven up to Chiu's house: Andrew Cheung, interview by Jodi Kantor, July 2017.
Amy Israel had recommended: Laura Madden, interviews by Jodi Kantor, July
2017–January 2019.
Allred's autobiography: Gloria Allred, *Fight Back and Win* (New York: HarperCollins,
2006); Gloria Allred, interviews by Megan Twohey, October 2016—spring 2019.
In 2011, she and a partner: Emily Steel, "How Bill O'Reilly Silenced His Accusers," *The
New York Times*, April 4, 2018, nytimes.com/2018/04/04/business/media/how-
bill-oreilly-silenced-his-accusers.html.
Allred was working on a settlement: Rebecca Davis O'Brien, "USA Gymnastics,
McKayla Maroney Had Confidentiality Agreement to Resolve Abuse Claims,"

The Wall Street Journal, December 20, 2017, wsj.com/articles/usa-gymnastics-reached-settlement-over-abuse-claims-with-gold-medalist-mckayla-maroney-1513791179; Will Hobson, "McKayla Maroney Sues USA Gymnastics, Saying It Tried to Buy Her Silence on Abuse," *The Washington Post*, December, 20, 2017, washingtonpost.com/sports/mckayla-maroney-sues-usa-gymnastics-saying-it-tried-to-buy-her-silence-on-abuse/2017/12/20/1e54b482-e5c8-11e7-a65d-1ac0fd7f097e_story.html.

in 2004, Allred's firm had also negotiated a settlement: Ashley Matthau, interviews by Megan Twohey, October 2017—spring 2019.

a group of consumer lawyers in California: Consumer Attorneys of California, caoc.org.

Then Allred stepped in: various participants on the call, interview by Megan Twohey, 2018.

CHAPTER FOUR: "POSITIVE REPUTATION MANAGEMENT"

his parents' Creole restaurant: Brett Anderson, "A History of the Baquets, New Orleans Restaurant Family: From the T-P Archives," NOLA.com, originally published July 20, 2004, republished May 15, 2014, nola.com/dining/2014/05/from_the_t-p_archives_a_short.html; Brett Anderson, "The Importance of Eddie's: The Late-great Baquet Family Restaurant, Remembered," NOLA.com, May 16, 2014, nola.com/dining/2014/05/the_importance_of_eddies_the_l.html.

Baquet was contacted by David Boies: information taken from Megan Twohey interviews, from 2017 through spring 2019, of Boies and those familiar with his representation of Harvey Weinstein, and emails and other records that included comments made by Boies from 2015 through 2017, as well as the following articles about him: Daniel Okrent, "Get Me Boies!," *Time*, December 25, 2000, content.time.com/time/world/article/0,8599,2047286,00.html; Andrew Rice, "The Bad, Good Lawyer: Was David Boies Just Doing Right by Harvey Weinstein? Or Did He Cross an Ethical Line?" *New York* magazine, September 30, 2018, nymag.com/intelligencer/2018/09/david-boies-harvey-weinstein-lawyer.html.

"I'm not calling as Harvey's lawyer": Dean Baquet, interviews by Megan Twohey and Jodi Kantor, 2018.

On August 3: Lanny Davis, interview by Megan Twohey and Jodi Kantor, August 3, 2017.

In 2002, the *New Yorker* writer: Auletta heard about the settlements while working on a profile of Harvey Weinstein. Ken Auletta, "Beauty and the Beast," *The New Yorker*, December 8, 2002, newyorker.com/magazine/2002/12/16/beauty-and-the-beast-2.

Auletta, David Remnick, the magazine's editor: Ken Auletta, Bob Weinstein, David Boies, interviews by Megan Twohey, 2019.

The producer had long relied on private detectives: Megan Twohey, Jodi Kantor, Susan Dominus, Jim Rutenberg, and Steve Eder, "Weinstein's Complicity Machine," *The New York Times*, December 5, 2017, nytimes.com/interactive/2017/12/05/us/harvey-weinstein-complicity.html.

Under the terms of a contract: Alana Goodman, "Harvey Weinstein's ORIGINAL contract with ex-Mossad agents ordered them to prove he was the victim of a 'negative campaign' in what was dubbed 'Operation Parachute'—spying on actresses, close friend designer Kenneth Cole and amfAR," *Daily Mail*, November 8, 2017, dailymail.co.uk/news/article-5062195/Harvey-Weinstein-agreed-pay-1-3m-ex-Mossad-agents.html.

Seth Freedman, a British freelance journalist: Megan Twohey and Jodi Kantor interviews of McGowan, Kendall, and others who were contacted by Seth Freedman in 2016 and 2017, and emails sent by Freedman.

Black Cube went to work on Benjamin Wallace: Benjamin Wallace, interview by Megan Twohey, 2018, and 2016 emails between Wallace and Seth Freedman.

By May 2017: Ronan Farrow, "Harvey Weinstein's Army of Spies," *The New Yorker*, November 6, 2017, newyorker.com/news/news-desk/harvey-weinsteins-army-of-spies.

Boies helped renegotiate Weinstein's contract with Black Cube: "Read: The Contract between a Private Security Firm and One of Harvey Weinstein's Lawyers," *The New Yorker*, November 6, 2017, newyorker.com/sections/news/read-the-contract-between-a-private-security-firm-and-one-of-harvey-weinsteins-lawyers.

Jodi received a series: "Diana Filip," email to Jodi Kantor, August 8, 2017. The associated website, Reuben Capital Partners, has been stripped; screenshots of the website were published. Alana Goodman, "EXCLUSIVE: The SPY Who Duped Rose McGowan UNMASKED! This is the blonde Israeli military veteran who worked undercover for disgraced mogul Harvey Weinstein and tricked the actress into sharing her memoirs," *Daily Mail*, November 8, 2017, dailymail.co.uk/news/article-5064027/Israeli-military-vet-duped-Rose-McGowan-revealed.html.

profile of Gloria Allred and Lisa Bloom: Alexandra Pechman, "Gloria Allred and Lisa Bloom Are the Defenders of Women in 2017," *W*, July 21, 2017, wmagazine.com/story/gloria-allred-lisa-bloom-donald-trump-blac-chyna-lawyer.

she had first become suspicious: Stephen Feller, "Trump Rape Accuser Cancels Press Conference after Death Threats," *United Press International*, November 3, 2016, upi.com/Top_News/US/2016/11/03/Trump-rape-accuser-cancels-press-conference-after-death-threats/2381478150421.

Bloom acknowledged that she solicited money: Kenneth P. Vogel, "Partisans, Wielding Money, Begin Seeking to Exploit Harassment Claim," *The New York Times*, December 31, 2017, nytimes.com/2017/12/31/us/politics/sexual-harassment-politics-partisanship.html.

Bloom denied ever pressuring: Lisa Bloom, interview by Jodi Kantor and Megan Twohey, 2019; Lisa Bloom email to Megan Twohey, June 2019.

One client, Tamara Holder: Tamara Holder, interviews by Megan Twohey, summer 2018—spring 2019; emails between Tamara Holder and Lisa Bloom; Lloyd Grove, "Clients Turn on 'Champion for Women' Lisa Bloom after Her Scorched-earth Crusade for Harvey Weinstein," *The Daily Beast*, October 26, 2017, thedailybeast.com/lisa-bloom-has-files-on-rose-mcgowans-history-inside-her-scorched-earth-crusade-for-harvey-weinstein; Emily Steel, "Fox Is Said to Settle with Former Contributor over Sexual Assault Claims," *The New York Times*, March 8, 2017, nytimes.com/2017/03/08/business/fox-news-roger-ailes-sexual-assault-settlement.html.

an unusual financial transaction involving Weinstein: Megan Twohey's amfAR reporting included interviews of amfAR board members, including its then chairman Kenneth Cole, Harvey Weinstein, David Boies, Charles Prince, and others with knowledge of the $600,000 raised at an amfAR charity auction that flowed to *Finding Neverland* investors. It also included emails and other documents from 2015 to 2017 that outlined the financial transaction, concern about the transaction among certain members of amfAR's staff and board, and how Weinstein responded to attempts to investigate it; Megan Twohey, "Tumult after AIDS Fund-Raiser Supports Harvey Weinstein Production," *The New York Times*, September 23, 2017, nytimes.com/2017/09/23/nyregion/harvey-weinstein-charity.html.

Megan was meeting Tom Ajamie: Tom Ajamie, interviews by Megan Twohey, summer
    2017–spring 2019.
Bloom had already been working with the producer: December 2016 billing records
    from Lisa Bloom's law firm, the Bloom Firm.
tracking their social media accounts: Sara Ness, Draft Report submitted to Harvey
    Weinstein, July 2017.

CHAPTER FIVE: A COMPANY'S COMPLICITY

To keep the dialogue over email going: Irwin Reiter emails to Jodi Kantor, September
    2017.
On Monday night, September 18: Irwin Reiter, interviews by Jodi Kantor and Megan
    Twohey, September 2017–May 2019.
By her second day of work: from emails and other internal Weinstein Company records
    from 2014 and 2015.
"She said he was very persistent": ibid.
Shari pressed forward: Shari Reiter, interview by Jodi Kantor, October 25, 2018.
Rehal was Weinstein's personal assistant: Sandeep Rehal, interviews by Jodi Kantor,
    November 2018.
$2.5 million in 2015: Harvey Weinstein's contract with The Weinstein Company.
was having eerily similar conversations: Michelle Franklin, interviews by Jodi Kantor,
    2017–19.
On the afternoon of September 19: Harvey Weinstein, Jason Lilien, Lanny Davis,
    Charlie Prince, Roberta Kaplan, and Karen Duffy, interview by Megan Twohey
    and Rebecca Corbett, September 19, 2017.
"I'm worse": Harvey Weinstein, interview by Jodi Kantor, September 19, 2017.
eager to see him charged: Megan Twohey, James C. McKinley Jr., Al Baker, and William
    K. Rashbaum, "For Weinstein, a Brush with the Police, Then No Charges," *The
    New York Times*, October 15, 2017, nytimes.com/2017/10/15/nyregion/harvey-
    weinstein-new-york-sex-assault-investigation.html.
Weinstein paid Gutierrez: Megan Twohey interviews of people familiar with the
    settlement and internal Weinstein Company records from 2015.
copy of the audio recording: Ronan Farrow, "Harvey Weinstein's Secret Settlements,"
    The New Yorker, November 21, 2017, newyorker.com/news/news-desk/
    harvey-weinsteins-secret-settlements.
No one had more incentive to hold Weinstein accountable: based on Megan Twohey
    interviews in 2018 and 2019 of Bob Weinstein, Megan Twohey and Jodi Kantor
    interviews of those who worked with him, as well as emails and other internal
    Weinstein Company records.
When Harvey Weinstein needed money: Megan Twohey interview of Bob
    Weinstein; Ronan Farrow, "Harvey Weinstein's Secret Settlements,"
    The New Yorker, November 21, 2017, newyorker.com/news/news-desk/
    harvey-weinsteins-secret-settlements.
One day in 2010 or 2011: Bob Weinstein, interview by Megan Twohey, 2018; Irwin
    Reiter, interviews by Jodi Kantor, 2017–19.
Bob sent David Boies an email: Bob Weinstein, email to David Boies, August 16, 2015.
But Lance Maerov, who had been appointed: Lance Maerov interviews by Megan
    Twohey, September 2016—spring 2019; interviews of those who worked with
    Maerov; emails and other internal Weinstein Company records.

Rodgin Cohen, one of the most prominent corporate lawyers: H. Rodgin Cohen, email to
  Philip Richter, an attorney for The Weinstein Company board, September 4, 2015.
The New York Attorney General's Office: Megan Twohey and William K. Rashbaum,
  "Transactions Tied to Weinstein and AIDS Charity Are Under Investigation," *The
  New York Times*, November 2, 2017, nytimes.com/2017/11/02/nyregion/harvey-
  weinstein-amfar.html.
a long, detailed complaint: internal Weinstein Company records from 2015 and 2016.

CHAPTER SIX: "WHO ELSE IS ON THE RECORD?"

At the start of his newspaper career: Dean Baquet, interviews by Jodi Kantor and
  Megan Twohey, 2018.
When the call itself began: Harvey Weinstein, Charles Harder, Lisa Bloom, and Lanny
  Davis, interview by Jodi Kantor, Megan Twohey, and Rebecca Corbett, October 3,
  2017.
Harder had made a name: Eriq Gardner, "Ailes Media Litigator Charles Harder
  on His Improbable Rise with Clients Melania Trump and Hulk Hogan,"
  Hollywood Reporter, September 22, 2016, hollywoodreporter.com/thr-esq/
  ailes-media-litigator-charles-harder-930963.
He had represented Roger Ailes: Brian Stelter, "Roger Ailes Enlists Lawyer behind
  Hulk Hogan and Melania Trump Suits," CNN Money, September 5, 2016, money.
  cnn.com/2016/09/05/media/roger-ailes-charles-harder/index.html.
After he negotiated a $2.9 million settlement: Tom Hamburger, "Melania Trump
  Missed Out on 'Once-in-a-Lifetime Opportunity' to Make Millions, Lawsuit
  Says," *The Washington Post*, February 7, 2017, washingtonpost.com/
  politics/melania-trump-missed-out-on-once-in-a-lifetime-opportunity-
  to-make-millions-lawsuit-says/2017/02/06/3654f070-ecd0-11e6-9973-
  c5efb7ccfb0d_story.html?utm_term=.1f8e8f635b8c&tid=a_inl_manual;
  Emily Hell, "When They Go Low, Melania Trump Calls Her Lawyers," *The
  Washington Post*, January 30, 2019, washingtonpost.com/lifestyle/style/
  when-they-go-low-melania-trump-calls-her-lawyers/2019/01/30/d3892a1e-
  240a-11e9-ad53-824486280311_story.html?utm_term=.09e90f097c14; Glenn
  Feishman, "Trump Hires Harder, Hulk Hogan's Gawker-Toppling Lawyer in
  Dispute against Omarosa," *Fortune*, August 14, 2018, fortune.com/2018/08/14/
  trump-charles-harder-gawker-lawyer-hulk-hogan-omarosa.
"the very notion of a free press": Jason Zengerle, "Charles Harder, the Lawyer
  Who Killed Gawker, Isn't Done Yet," *GQ*, November 17, 2016, gq.com/story/
  charles-harder-gawker-lawyer.
"it's going to be bad": Lance Maerov, David Boies, and David Glasser, interviews by
  Megan Twohey, 2018 and 2019.
"We can nip at it around the edges": Lisa Bloom, email to Harvey Weinstein, Lanny
  Davis, Charles Harder, and David Boies, October 4, 2017.

CHAPTER SEVEN: "THERE WILL BE A MOVEMENT"

....

Megan called David Glasser: David Glasser, interviews by Megan Twohey, October 2017 and spring 2019.

At 1:43 p.m., Team Weinstein's answer landed: Charles Harder, email to Diane Brayton, Arthur Sulzberger Jr., Dean Baquet, Jodi Kantor, and Megan Twohey, October 4, 2017.

At 3:33 p.m., McCraw forwarded the reporters: David McCraw, email to Charles Harder, October 4, 2017.

Jodi and Megan sat down to read about themselves: Brent Lang, Gene Maddaus, and Ramin Setoodeh, "Harvey Weinstein Lawyers Up for Bombshell *New York Times, New Yorker* Stories," *Variety*, October 4, 2017, variety.com/2017/film/ news/harvey-weinstein-sexual-new-york-times-1202580605; Kim Masters, Chris Gardner, "Harvey Weinstein Lawyers Battling *N.Y. Times, New Yorker* over Potentially Explosive Stories," *Hollywood Reporter*, October 4, 2017, hollywoodreporter.com/news/harvey-weinstein-lawyers-battling-ny-times-new-yorker-potentially-explosive-stories-1045724.

"My mom is just my mom": Gracie Allen, interview by Jodi Kantor, 2018.

Suddenly, Weinstein himself was on the phone: Harvey Weinstein and Lisa Bloom, interview by Jodi Kantor and Megan Twohey, October 5, 2017.

Tolan pushed the button: Jodi Kantor and Megan Twohey, "Harvey Weinstein Paid Off Sexual Harassment Accusers for Decades," *The New York Times*, October 5, 2017, nytimes.com/2017/10/05/us/harvey-weinstein-harassment-allegations.html.

most of the directors would resign: Bruce Haring, "Fifth Weinstein Company Board Member Resigns, Leaving Three Remaining," *Deadline*, October 14, 2017, deadline.com/2017/10/fifth-weinstein-company-board-member-resigns-leaving-three-left-1202188563.

Jodi and Megan began hearing from so many women: the stories of Tomi-Ann Roberts, as well as Katherine Kendall, Dawn Dunning, and Judith Godrèche, were all depicted in *The New York Times* in the following weeks. Jodi Kantor and Rachel Abrams, "Gwyneth Paltrow, Angelina Jolie and Others Say Weinstein Harassed Them," *The New York Times*, October 10, 2017, nytimes.com/2017/10/10/us/ gwyneth-paltrow-angelina-jolie-harvey-weinstein.html; the stories of Hope d'Amore and Cynthia Burr were depicted thereafter. Ellen Gabler, Megan Twohey, and Jodi Kantor, "New Accusers Expand Harvey Weinstein Sexual Assault Claims Back to '70s," *The New York Times*, October 30, 2017, nytimes. com/2017/10/30/us/harvey-weinstein-sexual-assault-allegations.html.

Ronan Farrow was finishing: Ronan Farrow, "From Aggressive Overtures to Sexual Assault: Harvey Weinstein's Accusers Tell Their Stories," *The New Yorker*, October 10, 2017, newyorker.com/news/news-desk/from-aggressive-overtures-to-sexual-assault-harvey-weinsteins-accusers-tell-their-stories.

when Megan later revealed in the paper: Nicole Pelletiere, "Harvey Weinstein's Adviser, Lisa Bloom, Speaks Out: 'There was misconduct,'" ABC, October 6, 2017, abcnews.go.com/Entertainment/harvey-weinsteins-adviser-lisa-bloom-speaks-misconduct/story?id=50321561; Megan Twohey and Johanna Barr, "Lisa Bloom, Lawyer Advising Harvey Weinstein, Resigns amid Criticism from Board Members," *The New York Times*, October 7, 2017, nytimes.com/2017/10/07/ business/lisa-bloom-weinstein-attorney.html.

CHAPTER EIGHT: AFTERWARD

....

"He's now experiencing all the things he's put everybody else through": Melena Ryzik, "Weinstein in Handcuffs Is a 'Start to Justice' for His Accusers," *The New York Times*, October 25, 2018, nytimes.com/2018/05/25/nyregion/metoo-accusers-harvey-weinstein.html.

Brafman gave a radio interview: "Defending 'Brilliant' Harvey Weinstein," BBC, June 15, 2018, bbc.co.uk/programmes/p06b4pjp.

twelve women: This chapter is based on audio recordings of the group interview that took place over two days.

the first of several women: Matthew Garrahan, "Harvey Weinstein: How Lawyers Kept a Lid on Sexual Harassment Claims," *Financial Times*, October 23, 2017, ft.com/content/1dc8a8ae-b7e0-11e7-8c12-5661783e5589.

a public case against confidential settlements: Holly Watt, "Harvey Weinstein Aide Tells of 'Morally Lacking' Non-disclosure Deal," *The Guardian*, March 28, 2018, theguardian.com/film/2018/mar/28/harvey-weinstein-assistant-zelda-perkins-i-was-trapped-in-a-vortex-of-fear; House of Commons Women and Equalities Committee, "Sexual Harassment in the Workplace, Fifth Report of Session 2017–2019," *House of Commons*, July 18, 2018, publications.parliament.uk/pa/cm201719/cmselect/cmwomeq/725/725.pdf.

Kim Lawson, a twenty-five-year-old: Kim Lawson, interviews by Jodi Kantor, 2018–19.

Another participant, Christine Blasey Ford: Christine Blasey Ford, interviews by Megan Twohey, December 2018—May 2019, and written communication between Ford and her friends, members of the Senate Judiciary Committee, and one of her lawyers. The paper in question can be found at researchgate.net/publication/327287729_Attenuation_of_Antidepressant_Effects_of_Ketamine_by_Opioid_Receptor_Antagonism.

run for a seat in the state legislature: Matthew Haag, "Rachel Crooks, Who Accused Trump of Sexual Assault, Wins Legislative Primary," *The New York Times*, May 9, 2018, nytimes.com/2018/05/09/us/politics/rachel-crooks-ohio.html.

more than eighty women had already come forward: Sara M. Moniuszko and Cara Kelly, "Harvey Weinstein Scandal: A Complete List of the 87 Accusers," *USA Today*, October 27, 2017, usatoday.com/story/life/people/2017/10/27/weinstein-scandal-complete-list-accusers/804663001.

TIPS ON
CHASING THE TRUTH

UNCOVER ABUSES

Whether you are part of a formal investigations department, like ours at the *New York Times*, or you are a freelance reporter working on your own, the goal of investigative journalism is to reveal abuses of power that are causing harm to individuals or to the wider public. Megan was moved to join Jodi on this investigation because of clues that Weinstein's alleged abuse hurt women, caused them career harm, and also had far wider implications for how women were treated in the workplace. If you are scrupulous about your reporting, the First Amendment to the US Constitution will protect your work.

FOLLOW THE FACTS

You are in a pact with your readers: they can believe in your work because you have committed to the follow the facts wherever they lead. Your feelings may spur you to pursue an investigation on a given topic, or add to its urgency, but they shouldn't color your interpretation of the facts. Bill O'Reilly's suggestion that Megan's reporting was questionable because she is a feminist was nonsense. It was simply a way to distract readers from her rock-solid findings. Similarly, if you feel strongly about protecting the environment, you may be interested in investigating a factory operating along a local waterway. But to be taken seriously, you have to go into your investigation with an open mind. If your reporting

is reliable and sound, advocates and policymakers
may grab the ball and push for specific solutions to the
problems you have uncovered. Investigative journalists
follow facts, not an activist's agenda.

BE SPECIFIC AND PRECISE

Your investigation should include names, dates, legal and
financial information, on-the-record interviews, and
documents. Without those ingredients an investigation
will lack bite, as Judd's 2015 interview with *Variety*
proved, and can even do harm, as was the case with the
factually flawed *Rolling Stone* story about sexual assault
at the University of Virginia. Impact in journalism
comes from specificity—proof, patterns, and stories that
come to life. In investigative journalism, knowing about
incriminating documents is good; seeing them is excellent;
and having copies is best.

FIND SOURCES

Start by researching your topic. To look for sources with
firsthand experience, you can search through public
records like Nexis and social media sites like LinkedIn.
But it's also important to network, asking for introductions
from experts and intermediaries. If your investigation is
particularly sensitive, you may have to find back channels
to contact the most relevant sources. In our case, we took
all kinds of circuitous routes to reach actresses directly

because we thought it would hurt our investigation to approach their agents or managers. When you have gotten a source's cell phone number, you've achieved a small victory—like when Megan got the cell number of a former Miramax employee who had suddenly disappeared.

PREPARE FOR INTERVIEWS

Do as much research as possible before contacting sources, write down your questions for them, and think through how you might be able to get them to talk. For example, heading into her first careful outreach to Rose McGowan, Jodi knew she needed to establish her credibility and authority.

Put yourself in the shoes of your sources and think about all the different ways they would say no, until you hit upon an argument that will be convincing to them. After years of experience reporting on victims of sexual abuse, Megan had developed an approach that was particularly effective: "I can't change what happened to you in the past, but together we may be able to use your experience to help protect other people."

RESEARCH YOUR SOURCES

You have to make sure your sources will be credible—to protect the sources themselves and your publication from potential backlash. That's why we relied on *Times* colleagues to examine the backgrounds of Ashley Judd and Ambra Battilana Gutierrez to make sure there were no surprises that could be used against the women or the paper.

If sources approach you, make sure to do your research on them too. Like Lisa Bloom's early outreach to Jodi, or that of "Diana Filip," these sources might have an agenda for contacting you. Engaging with them might offer more clues for your investigation; just make sure you are careful in those interactions to protect what you are working on. Sometimes these conversations can be useful, as when Megan noted that people who have something to hide often give themselves away. This convinced our bosses to allow for an initial on-background conversation with Lanny Davis.

ESTABLISH THE GROUND RULES

When you connect with a potential source, first introduce yourself and describe the story you are working on. Then settle on ground rules with that source. Both of you have to agree to the ground rules for them to be in effect. Sources may be:

- On the record, which means you can publish their quotes along with their names. If possible, you should still try to corroborate, or support, whatever information an on-the-record source gives you with another source.
- On background, which means you can use the information they tell you without using their names or identifying information. You need at least two sources to confirm on-background information.

- Off the record, which means you can't use the information they provide or quote them unless you're also able to obtain the information from somewhere else. This is still helpful because you'll know what information to search for elsewhere.

BE UP FRONT WITH YOUR SOURCES

There are going to be times when you don't use sources' names at all, like to protect children who are victims of sexual abuse. There will also be times when you use names even if the source doesn't want you to, as was the case with Lauren O'Connor. She hadn't provided us with her memo—she wasn't our source for it—and we made that clear in the article. But we had gotten a hold of it, and it was crucial backup for our investigation.

Before publication, run everything in the article by your sources. For Weinstein's alleged victims, we did this to make sure they were comfortable with what we were publishing and that we had the details absolutely correct. For Weinstein, we did it to be fair and give him a chance to respond (more on this below). We have a "no surprises" rule: if your name is going to be in our story, you'll have heard from us first to discuss the material.

RECORD YOUR CONVERSATIONS

It's important to record your conversations with an audio recorder or app if possible and do careful note-taking.

When you record, you need to get permission from your source, just as we did with Lanny Davis when he came in for his first on-background meeting with us.

DOCUMENT YOUR FINDINGS

As much as possible, look for documents to back up your investigations. In our case, it was seeing letters, emails, copies of legal settlements, and financial records. When Zelda Perkins read her settlement aloud to Jodi, that was good; when Irwin Reiter let her copy the Lauren O'Connor memo, that was best. That kind of evidence prevents the powerful figure you are examining from debunking your investigation as hearsay. Whether or not documents are available, try to get as many sources as possible. In our case, no one had ever before nailed the Weinstein story, so we had to do it cleanly.

SHOW UP

Sometimes, the only way to track down a source is in person and by surprise. That's what Megan did when she showed up at the home of a former Miramax executive and again at the home of a former employee's mom. Jodi did the same when she appeared in Rowena Chiu's driveway. While there's the risk of scaring off or annoying the source—as when another former executive slammed her door in our faces—you'll also be making an impression and showing your potential source just how committed you are to the investigation. Come prepared with a note explaining your visit, if it turns out that no one is home.

DOUBLE-CHECK

Investigative journalists must scrutinize, verify, check, and question information, like the former editor of Megan's who had a sign on his desk warning reporters: IF YOUR MOTHER TELLS YOU SHE LOVES YOU, CHECK IT OUT. And when you are checking out a claim in your report, be sure to confirm with your sources that you can use them to corroborate, as Megan did when she asked the executive David Glasser if she could use him as a second source on the number of settlements Weinstein had reached with women.

BE FAIR

Always present your findings to the subjects of your investigation for their comment and make sure to incorporate their answers into your article. Print their denials or apologies. If they refuse to comment, note that in your piece, and if they can refute—meaning truly disprove with their own documents—any of the allegations, remove those claims from your report. They shouldn't be surprised by what you publish.

And just beforehand, be sure to warn your sources that you're approaching the target of the investigation and that they should be prepared for blowback. This is why we reached out to Perkins, Madden, and others before we went to Weinstein with their allegations.

GO OFF TOPIC

If, in the course of your investigation, you stumble upon another abuse of power, think about whether or not it's worth pursuing as a related part of your original investigation. Megan's hunch to follow leads of suspicious financial transactions in Weinstein's charity work ended up supporting our investigation about his sexual harassment and abuse. It gave her a window into how he operated that helped us strengthen our investigation, and her published report encouraged other sources to speak with us.

MOVE FAST

While you have to make sure your reporting is double and triple checked, well documented, and fair, you also have to move fast. For one, if powerful targets find out about the investigation before you reach them for comment, they may try to foil your investigation. This was a concern from the moment that Lisa Bloom first reached out to Jodi and she realized that Weinstein was on her trail. Also, other reporters may be looking into the same matter—like Ronan Farrow was—and you want to be the first to break the story.

Each investigation will present its own sensitivities. In the case of the Weinstein investigation, we had to act with special care, as many of our sources were victims of abuse. It's hard to know when to keep pursuing a source and when to walk away, but push as far as you can whenever you can, strategically. That's why Jodi repeatedly texted Gwyneth Paltrow to go on the record. In the end, Paltrow did not, but Jodi's persistence did work with Ashley Judd and other women.

HARVEY WEINSTEIN PAID OFF SEXUAL HARASSMENT ACCUSERS FOR DECADES

By Jodi Kantor and Megan Twohey

Oct. 5, 2017

Two decades ago, the Hollywood producer Harvey Weinstein invited Ashley Judd to the Peninsula Beverly Hills hotel for what the young actress expected to be a business breakfast meeting. Instead, he had her sent up to his room, where he appeared in a bathrobe and asked if he could give her a massage or she could watch him shower, she recalled in an interview.

"How do I get out of the room as fast as possible without alienating Harvey Weinstein?" Ms. Judd said she remembers thinking.

1   In 2014, Mr. Weinstein invited Emily Nestor, who had worked just one day as a temporary employee, to the same hotel and made another offer: If she accepted his sexual advances, he would boost her career, according to accounts she provided to colleagues who sent them to Weinstein Company executives. The following year, once again at the Peninsula, a female assistant said Mr. Weinstein badgered her into giving him a massage while he was naked, leaving her "crying and very distraught," wrote a colleague, Lauren O'Connor, in a searing memo asserting sexual harassment and other misconduct by their boss.

1. Write a lede that draws on the most powerful findings of your reporting. In this case, we stacked similar on-the-record accounts of sexual misconduct that demonstrated a pattern of wrongdoing by Weinstein.

2. Documents strengthen an investigative story. Here we were showing readers that we obtained many. Getting a copy of the Lauren O'Connor memo from Irwin Reiter, Weinstein's corporate accountant of many years, was one of the most significant developments in our reporting. Cultivating Reiter as a source took time and care.

3. Never attribute a crucial finding, like the number of secret settlements that Weinstein paid, to a single anonymous source. Make sure you get a second source to corroborate it.

4. Another hallmark of investigative reporting is fairness. Before publishing a story, you must inform the subjects of everything you intend to say about them and give them an opportunity to comment and offer any evidence they might have that rebuts your findings. A subject should never be surprised by the content of a story.

"There is a toxic environment for women at this company," Ms. O'Connor said in the letter, addressed to several executives at the company run by Mr. Weinstein.

An investigation by The New York Times found previously undisclosed allegations against Mr. Weinstein stretching over nearly three decades, documented through interviews with current and former employees and film industry workers, as well as legal records, emails and internal documents from the businesses he has run, Miramax and the Weinstein Company.

2

During that time, after being confronted with allegations including sexual harassment and unwanted physical contact, <u>Mr. Weinstein has</u> **3** <u>reached at least eight settlements with women,</u> <u>according to two company officials speaking on the</u> <u>condition of anonymity.</u> Among the recipients, The Times found, were a young assistant in New York in 1990, an actress in 1997, an assistant in London in 1998, an Italian model in 2015 and Ms. O'Connor shortly after, according to records and those familiar with the agreements.

4 <u>In a statement to The Times on Thursday after-</u> <u>noon, Mr. Weinstein said:</u> "I appreciate the way I've behaved with colleagues in the past has caused a lot of pain, and I sincerely apologize for it. Though I'm trying to do better, I know I have a long way to go."

He added that he was working with therapists and planning to take a leave of absence to "deal with this issue head on."

Lisa Bloom, a lawyer advising Mr. Weinstein, said in a statement that "he denies many of the accusations as patently false." In comments to The Times earlier this week, Mr. Weinstein said that many claims in Ms. O'Connor's memo were "off base" and that they had parted on good terms.

Harvey Weinstein Paid Off Sexual Harassment Accusers for Decades

He and his representatives declined to comment on any of the settlements, including providing information about who paid them. But Mr. Weinstein said that in addressing employee concerns about workplace issues, "my motto is to keep the peace."

Ms. Bloom, who has been advising Mr. Weinstein over the last year on gender and power dynamics, called him "an old dinosaur learning new ways." She said she had "explained to him that due to the power difference between a major studio head like him and most others in the industry, whatever his motives, some of his words and behaviors can be perceived as inappropriate, even intimidating."

Though Ms. O'Connor had been writing only about a two-year period, her memo echoed other women's complaints. Mr. Weinstein required her to have casting discussions with aspiring actresses after they had private appointments in his hotel room, she said, her description matching those of other former employees.

She suspected that she and other female Weinstein employees, she wrote, were being used to facilitate liaisons with "vulnerable women who hope he will get them work."

The allegations piled up even as Mr. Weinstein helped define popular culture. He has collected six best-picture Oscars and turned out a number of touchstones, from the films "Sex, Lies, and Videotape," "Pulp Fiction" and "Good Will Hunting" to the television show "Project Runway." In public, he presents himself as a liberal lion, a champion of women and a winner of not just artistic but humanitarian awards.

5

5. Investigative journalism is about holding the powerful to account. It was important here to establish the power that Weinstein had.

In 2015, the year Ms. O'Connor wrote her memo, his company distributed "The Hunting Ground," a documentary about campus sexual assault. A longtime Democratic donor, he hosted a fund-raiser for Hillary Clinton in his Manhattan home last year. He employed Malia Obama, the oldest daughter of former President Barack Obama, as an intern this year, and recently helped endow a faculty chair at Rutgers University in Gloria Steinem's name. During the Sundance Film Festival in January, when Park City, Utah, held its version of nationwide women's marches, Mr. Weinstein joined the parade.

6. Many top executives who had worked for Weinstein refused to discuss him on the record. This former executive was an exception. His decision came at the very end of our investigation. Outraged to learn the extent of Weinstein's alleged abuses, he was finally prepared to share his perspective publicly.

"From the outside, it seemed golden—the Oscars, the success, the remarkable cultural impact," said Mark Gill, former president of Miramax Los Angeles when the company was owned by Disney. "But behind the scenes, it was a mess, and this was the biggest mess of all," he added, referring to Mr. Weinstein's treatment of women.

6

Dozens of Mr. Weinstein's former and current employees, from assistants to top executives, said they knew of inappropriate conduct while they worked for him. Only a handful said they ever confronted him.

Mr. Weinstein enforced a code of silence; employees of the Weinstein Company have contracts saying they will not criticize it or its leaders in a way that could harm its "business reputation" or "any employee's personal reputation," a recent document shows. And most of the women accepting payouts agreed to confidentiality clauses prohibiting them from speaking about the deals or the events that led to them.

Charles Harder, a lawyer representing Mr. Weinstein, said it was not unusual to enter into settlements to avoid lengthy and costly litigation. He added, "It's not evidence of anything." 8

At Fox News, where the conservative icons Roger E. Ailes and Bill O'Reilly were accused of harassment, women have received payouts well into the millions of dollars. But most of the women involved in the Weinstein agreements collected between roughly $80,000 and $150,000, according to people familiar with the negotiations.

In the wake of Ms. O'Connor's 2015 memo, some Weinstein Company board members and executives, including Mr. Weinstein's brother and longtime partner, Bob, 62, were alarmed about the allegations, according to several people who spoke on the condition of anonymity. In the end, though, board members were assured there was no need to investigate. After reaching a settlement with Mr.

7. The key to this story was getting sources to break their silence— in many cases silence that was legally binding. If you keep encountering people who refuse to speak in the course of your reporting, that can be a signficant clue. It's likely that something is being concealed, and it's important to keep digging.

8. More fairness: sprinkled here and throughout the piece are comments by Weinstein and his team addressing allegations.

Weinstein, Ms. O'Connor withdrew her complaint and thanked him for the career opportunity he had given her.

"The parties made peace very quickly," Ms. Bloom said.

Through her lawyer, Nicole Page, Ms. O'Connor declined to be interviewed. In the memo, she explained how unnerved she was by what she witnessed or encountered while a literary scout and production executive at the company. "I am just starting out in my career, and have been and remain fearful about speaking up," Ms. O'Connor wrote. "But remaining silent is causing me great distress."

In speaking out about her hotel episode, Ms. Judd said in a recent interview, "Women have been talking about Harvey amongst ourselves for a long time, and it's simply beyond time to have the conversation publicly."

A Common Narrative

Ms. Nestor, a law and business school student, accepted Mr. Weinstein's breakfast invitation at the Peninsula because she did not want to miss an opportunity, she later told colleagues. After she arrived, he offered to help her career while boasting about a series of famous actresses he claimed to have slept with, according to accounts that colleagues compiled after hearing her story and then sent on to company executives.

"She said he was very persistent and focused though she kept saying no for over an hour," one

9. We used the Lauren O'Connor memo in the story because it was valuable documentation of the pattern of abuse that we had uncovered. We also included a line saying that O'Connor had declined to be interviewed, making clear that she was not the one who had shared her memo with us.

9

internal document said. Ms. Nestor, who declined to comment for this article, refused his bargain, the records noted. "She was disappointed that he met with her and did not seem to be interested in her résumé or skill set." The young woman chose not to report the episode to human resources personnel, but the allegations came to management's attention through other employees.

Across the years and continents, accounts of Mr. Weinstein's conduct share a common narrative: Women reported to a hotel for what they thought were work reasons, only to discover that Mr. Weinstein, who has been married for most of three decades, sometimes seemed to have different interests. His home base was New York, but his rolling headquarters were luxury hotels: the Peninsula Beverly Hills and the Savoy in London, the Hôtel du Cap-Eden-Roc near the Cannes Film Festival in France and the Stein Eriksen Lodge near the Sundance Film Festival.

Working for Mr. Weinstein could mean getting him out of bed in the morning and doing "turndown duty" late at night, preparing him for sleep. Like the colleague cited in Ms. O'Connor's memo, some junior employees required to perform those tasks said they were disturbing.

In interviews, eight women described varying behavior by Mr. Weinstein: appearing nearly or fully naked in front of them, requiring them to be present while he bathed or repeatedly asking for a massage or initiating one himself. The women, typically in their early or middle 20s and hoping to get a toehold in the film industry, said he could switch course quickly—meetings and clipboards one moment, intimate comments the next. One woman advised a peer to wear a parka when summoned for duty as a layer of protection against unwelcome advances.

Laura Madden, a former employee who said Mr. Weinstein prodded her for massages at hotels in Dublin and London beginning in 1991, said he had a way of making anyone who objected feel like an outlier. "It was so manipulative," she said in an interview. "You constantly question yourself—am I the one who is the problem?"

"I don't know anything about that," Mr. Weinstein said.

Most women who told The Times that they experienced misconduct by Mr. Weinstein had never met one another. They range in age from early 20s to late 40s and live in different cities. Some said they did not report the behavior because there were no witnesses and they feared retaliation by Mr. Weinstein. Others said they felt embarrassed. But most confided in co-workers.

Ms. Madden later told Karen Katz, a friend and colleague in the acquisitions department, about Mr. Weinstein's overtures, including a time she locked herself in the bathroom of his hotel room, sobbing. "We were so young at the time," said Ms. Katz, now a documentary filmmaker. "We did not understand how wrong it was or how Laura should deal with it."

Others in the London office said the same. "I was pretty disturbed and angry," said Sallie Hodges, another former employee, recalling the accounts she

10. Laura Madden was the only former Weinstein employee to go on the record with her allegation of sexual misconduct. In doing so, she buttressed the allegations of other former employees who had made allegations against Weinstein who were legally prohibited from speaking out or too scared to.

heard from colleagues. "That's kind of the way things were."

The human resources operation was considered weak in New York and worse in London, so some employees banded together in solidarity. "If a female executive was asked to go to a meeting solo, she and a colleague would generally double up" so as not to be alone with Mr. Weinstein, recalled Mr. Gill, the former president of Miramax Los Angeles.

Many women who worked with Mr. Weinstein said they never experienced sexual harassment or knew of anyone who did, and recalled him as a boss who gave them valuable opportunities at young ages. Some described long and satisfying careers with him, praising him as a mentor and advocate.

But in interviews, some of the former employees who said they had troubling experiences with Mr. Weinstein asked a common question: How could allegations repeating the same pattern—young women, a powerful male producer, even some of the same hotels—have accumulated for almost three decades?

"It wasn't a secret to the inner circle," said Kathy DeClesis, Bob Weinstein's assistant in the early 1990s. She supervised a young woman who left the company abruptly after an encounter with Harvey Weinstein and who later received a settlement, according to several former employees.

Speaking up could have been costly. A job with Mr. Weinstein was a privileged perch at the nexus of money, fame and art, and plenty of his former assistants have risen high in Hollywood. He could

11. Fairness in investigative journalism goes beyond giving the subject an opportunity to comment. It's also about making sure that your story reflects the breadth of your findings, no matter how nuanced they may be.

be charming and generous: gift baskets, flowers, personal or career help and cash. At the Cannes Film Festival, according to several former colleagues, he sometimes handed out thousands of dollars as impromptu bonuses.

Mr. Weinstein was a volcanic personality, though, given to fits of rage and personal lashings of male and female employees alike. When a female guest of his had to wait for a hotel room upgrade, he yelled that Ms. O'Connor would be better off marrying a "fat, rich Jewish" man because she was probably just good for "being a wife" and "making babies," she wrote in her memo. (He added some expletives, she said.) His treatment of women was sometimes written off as just another form of toxicity, according to multiple former employees.

In the fall of 1998, a 25-year-old London assistant named Zelda Perkins confronted Mr. Weinstein. According to former colleagues, she and several co-workers had been regularly subjected to inappropriate requests or comments in hotel rooms, and she was particularly concerned about the treatment of another woman in the office. She told Mr. Weinstein that he had to stop, according to the former colleagues, and that she would go public or initiate legal action unless he changed his behavior.

Steve Hutensky, one of Miramax's entertainment lawyers, was dispatched to London to negotiate a settlement with Ms. Perkins and her lawyer. He declined to comment for this article.

Ms. Perkins, now a theater producer in London, also declined to comment for this article, saying that she could not discuss her work at Miramax or whether she had entered into any agreements.

Months after the settlement, Mr. Weinstein triumphed at the Oscars, with "Life Is Beautiful" and "Shakespeare in Love" winning 10 awards. A few years later, Mr. Weinstein, who had produced a series of British-themed movies, was made a Commander of the British Empire, an honorary title just short of knighthood.

'Coercive Bargaining'

For actors, a meeting with Mr. Weinstein could yield dazzling rewards: scripts, parts, award campaigns, magazine coverage, influence on lucrative endorsement deals. He knew how to blast small films to box office success, and deliver polished dramas like "The King's Speech" and popular attractions like the "Scary Movie" franchise. Mr. Weinstein's films helped define femininity, sex and romance, from Catherine Zeta-Jones in "Chicago" to Jennifer Lawrence in "Silver Linings Playbook."

But movies were also his private leverage. When Mr. Weinstein invited Ms. Judd to breakfast in Beverly Hills, she had been shooting the thriller "Kiss the Girls" all night, but the meeting seemed too important to miss. After arriving at the hotel lobby, she was surprised to learn that they would be talking in his suite; she decided to order cereal, she said, so the food would come quickly and she could leave.

Mr. Weinstein soon issued invitation after invitation, she said. Could he give her a massage?

When she refused, he suggested a shoulder rub. She rejected that too, she recalled. He steered her toward a closet, asking her to help pick out his clothing for the day, and then toward the bathroom. Would she watch him take a shower? she remembered him saying.

"I said no, a lot of ways, a lot of times, and he always came back at me with some new ask," Ms. Judd said. "It was all this bargaining, this coercive bargaining."

To get out of the room, she said, she quipped that if Mr. Weinstein wanted to touch her, she would first have to win an Oscar in one of his movies. She recalled feeling "panicky, trapped," she said in the interview. "There's a lot on the line, the cachet that came with Miramax."

Not long afterward, she related what had happened to her mother, the singer Naomi Judd, who confirmed their conversation to a Times reporter. Years later, Ashley Judd appeared in two Weinstein films without incident, she said. In 2015, she shared an account of the episode in the hotel room with "Variety" without naming the man involved.

In 1997, Mr. Weinstein reached a previously undisclosed settlement with Rose McGowan, then a 23-year-old actress, after an episode in a hotel room during the Sundance Film Festival. The $100,000 settlement was "not to be construed as an admission" by Mr. Weinstein, but intended to "avoid litigation and buy peace," according to the legal document, which was reviewed by The Times. Ms. McGowan had just appeared in the slasher film

12. Judd had been reluctant to go on the record in our story. That's because when she had written about her experience in the 2015 article, with a veiled reference to Weinstein, nothing had changed. Her concern helped guide our reporting; we knew we needed to establish a pattern of behavior through documents and on-the-record sources.

13. Legal records are among the most valuable documents in investigative reporting!

12

13

"Scream" and would later star in the television show "Charmed." She declined to comment.

Increased Scrutiny

Just months before Ms. O'Connor wrote her memo, a young female employee quit after complaining of being forced to arrange what she believed to be assignations for Mr. Weinstein, according to two people familiar with her departure. The woman, who asked not to be identified to protect her privacy, said a nondisclosure agreement prevented her from commenting.

Soon, complaints about Mr. Weinstein's behavior prompted the board of his company to take notice.

In March 2015, Mr. Weinstein had invited Ambra Battilana, an Italian model and aspiring actress, to his TriBeCa office on a Friday evening to discuss her career. Within hours, she called the police. Ms. Battilana told them that Mr. Weinstein had grabbed her breasts after asking if they were real and put his hands up her skirt, the police report says.

The claims were taken up by the New York Police Department's Special Victims Squad and splashed across the pages of tabloids, along with reports that the woman had worked with investigators to secretly record a confession from Mr. Weinstein. The Manhattan district attorney's office later declined to bring charges.

But Mr. Weinstein made a payment to Ms. Battilana, according to people familiar with the settlement, speaking on the condition of anonymity about the confidential agreement.

The public nature of the episode concerned some executives and board members of the Weinstein Company. (Harvey and Bob Weinstein together own 42 percent of the privately held business.) When several board members pressed Mr. Weinstein about it, he insisted that the woman had set him up, colleagues recalled.

Ms. Battilana had testified in court proceedings against associates of former Prime Minister Silvio Berlusconi of Italy who are accused of procuring women for alleged sex parties, and the Italian news media also reported that, years ago, Ms. Battilana accused a septuagenarian boyfriend of sexual harassment, a complaint that was apparently dismissed. Ms. Battilana did not respond to requests for comment. Her lawyer, Mauro Rufini, could not be reached for comment.

After the episode, Lance Maerov, a board member, said he successfully pushed for a code of behavior for the company that included detailed language about sexual harassment.

Then Ms. O'Connor's memo hit, with page after page of detailed accusations. In describing the experiences of women at the company, including her own, she wrote, "The balance of power is me: 0, Harvey Weinstein: 10."

She was a valued employee—Mr. Weinstein described her as "fantastic," "a great person," "a brilliant executive"—so the complaint rattled top executives, including Bob Weinstein. When

14. This story got bigger when we were able to show that it went beyond a pattern of behavior by one man. That other people in power at his company were aware of allegations against Weinstein. And that some tried—and failed—to do something about it. In seeking to probe the question of complicity, it was crucial to develop sources within the company and on its board. Lance Maerov, a board member, had an incentive to speak to us when he realized that we had the Lauren O'Connor memo. He wanted to explain why the board did nothing about it.

14

the board was notified of it by email, Mr. Maerov insisted that an outside lawyer determine whether the allegations were true, he said in an interview.

But the inquiry never happened. Mr. Weinstein had reached a settlement with Ms. O'Connor, and there was no longer anything to investigate.

"Because this matter has been resolved and no further action is required, I withdraw my complaint," Ms. O'Connor wrote in an email to the head of human resources six days after sending her memo. She also wrote a letter to Mr. Weinstein thanking him for the opportunity to learn about the entertainment industry.

Rachel Abrams and William K. Rashbaum contributed reporting. Grace Ashford contributed research.

A version of this article appears in print on Oct. 6, 2017, Section A, Page 1 of the New York edition with the headline: Sexual Misconduct Claims Trail a Hollywood Mogul

INDEX